Praise for
Awakening

"I began fasting as a teenager simply out of a hunger for more of God. It was during a fast that I experienced an awakening. This moment propelled me into my calling to preach the gospel. Through these pages, Pastor Stovall Weems challenges the reader to believe God for a Christian life that is not just focused on the glory of someday but on the glory of today—living in His presence, awakened by His Spirit, and walking in His purpose. Your awakening is not far off! This book will give you the keys to your breakthrough."

> —JENTEZEN FRANKLIN, senior pastor of Free Chapel and *New York Times* best-selling author of *Fasting: Opening the Door to a Deeper, More Intimate, More Powerful Relationship with God*

"There is an awakening simmering in this generation. It's an awakening of power, integrity, and a wholehearted pursuit of Jesus. Nobody embodies these characteristics more than my friend Stovall Weems. If you want your soul to be ignited with the passion it was created to possess, you need to read this book."

> —STEVEN FURTICK, lead pastor of Elevation Church and author of *Sun Stand Still*

"In order to effectively lead others as a church leader, one of the most important things you will ever do is learn to lead yourself well. In *Awakening*, Stovall Weems shares some valuable principles to help ensure that *your* spiritual leadership remains healthy, vibrant, and full of the life and fire of God. The message of *Awakening* is one that is vital for every church leader, and I'm so glad Stovall is sharing these principles with the body of Christ. *Awakening* will not only encourage you today, but it will also prepare you for tomorrow."

> —JOHN C. MAXWELL, author, speaker, and founder of EQUIP Leadership Inc.

"Passion. Zeal. Authenticity. These are the characteristics that should describe the life of one who loves God. I want them to describe mine, and if this book is in your hands, then you most likely want the same. There is no one better suited for giving us insight into how to obtain all three than Stovall Weems. His enthusiasm for spiritual things is genuine and contagious. Choosing to read these pages will dramatically transform your walk with the Lord. So wipe your tired spiritual eyes and prepare for your awakening."

—PRISCILLA SHIRER, author and Bible teacher

"This world will never be changed by passive people. All the greatest accomplishments of humanity have come about through passionate people who weren't afraid of what others thought or spoke of them. *Awakening*, my friend Stovall Weems's book, is a wake-up call to every Christian to get off the sidelines, discover the passion inside of them, and live the extraordinary life God calls them to live."

—JOHN BEVERE, author of *Extraordinary: The Life You're Meant to Live,* speaker, and cofounder of Messenger International

"We know deep down in our hearts that we really are meant to live in an exciting, passionate, ongoing, head-over-heels relationship with Jesus, but many of us just don't know how to maintain it. In *Awakening*, Stovall Weems shows us how easy it really is! Thanks for reawakening my soul through this life-changing book!"

—ROBERT MORRIS, senior pastor of Gateway Church

"If you want to experience God in a rich, powerful, and passionate way every day, then without a doubt you will want to read *Awakening*. Knowing God through prayer and fasting can be something that changes you forever. My friend Stovall lives this way daily, and he is revealing secrets that I've never seen or read before. We all need this book, and we need it now."

—RICK BEZET, lead pastor of New Life Church, Central Arkansas

"In His own words, Jesus said that He came to earth so that we could experience an abundant life. In other words, the personal and intimate relationship we can have with God should usher in nothing short of extraordinary experiences every single day. Yet far too often, Christians find their relationship with God lacking something. In the pages of *Awakening*, my close friend Stovall Weems unpacks the power and potential of a revitalized and reenergized relationship with God. And he shows us exactly what it takes for us to remain alert and expectant in our faith so that we will encounter the extraordinary every day!"

—ED YOUNG, pastor of Fellowship Church and author
of *Outrageous, Contagious Joy*

"In *Awakening*, Stovall Weems unpacks the timeless truth that there is power in praying and fasting. Your relationship with God will receive a jolt like you've never experienced before with the practical teaching that is revealed throughout this book. As you read, my prayer is that you'll find yourself more excited than ever before about the present and future of your life."

—DINO RIZZO, lead pastor of Healing Place Church

"Stovall Weems is a modern-day prophet. In this groundbreaking book he helps to awaken us to the fact that God wants us to live a radical, passionate Christianity. Jesus did not come to give us a religious obligation but abundant life. I was left with a renewed love and passion for Jesus and a clearer understanding of the privilege and purpose of prayer and fasting. This man lives this message, and read it at your own risk. You will never be the same."

—CHRISTINE CAINE, director of Equip and Empower Ministries
and founder of The A21 Campaign

"One of the things I love most is seeing people have a 'get it' moment that changes their life. This book will do that for you. I love the fact that it is both inspirational and informational. Stovall's passion has impacted my life, and through this book, it will impact your life too. Read it and experience an awakening. As Stovall puts it, 'After an awakening, life is never the same.'"

—JOHN SIEBELING, lead pastor of The Life Church,
  Memphis, Tennessee

"At a time when the moral fabric of our generation is eroding and people's hearts are further and further away from God, Stovall Weems calls us back to God with all of our hearts. In this powerful and timely book, you'll be both inspired and informed about the life-transforming power of prayer and fasting. This is a must-read at any stage in your walk with God."

—CHRIS HODGES, senior pastor of Church of the Highlands,
  Birmingham, Alabama

AWAKENING

AWAKENING

A New Approach to Faith, Fasting, and Spiritual Freedom

21 Days
to
Revolutionize
your
Relationship
with
God

STOVALL WEEMS

WATERBROOK
PRESS

AWAKENING
PUBLISHED BY WATERBROOK PRESS
12265 Oracle Boulevard, Suite 200
Colorado Springs, Colorado 80921

This book is not intended as a substitute for the advice and care of your physician, and as with any fasting, fitness, diet, or nutrition plan, you should use proper discretion, in consultation with your physician, in utilizing the information presented. The author and the publisher expressly disclaim responsibility for any adverse effects that may result from the use or application of the information contained in this book.

All Scripture quotations, unless otherwise indicated, are taken from the New King James Version®. Copyright © 1982 by Thomas Nelson Inc. Used by permission. All rights reserved. Scripture quotations marked (AMP) are taken from the Amplified Bible. Copyright © 1954, 1958, 1962, 1964, 1965, 1987 by The Lockman Foundation. Used by permission. Scripture quotations marked (KJV) are taken from the King James Version. Scripture quotations marked (MSG) are taken from The Message by Eugene H. Peterson. Copyright © 1993, 1994, 1995, 1996, 2000, 2001, 2002. Used by permission of NavPress Publishing Group. All rights reserved. Scripture quotations marked (NIV) are taken from the Holy Bible, New International Version®. NIV®. Copyright © 1973, 1978, 1984 by Biblica Inc.™ Used by permission of Zondervan. All rights reserved worldwide. www.zondervan.com. Scripture quotations marked (NLT) are taken from the Holy Bible, New Living Translation, copyright © 1996, 2004. Used by permission of Tyndale House Publishers Inc., Wheaton, Illinois 60189. All rights reserved.

ISBN 978-0-307-45953-4
ISBN 978-0-307-45954-1 (electronic)

Cover design by Kelly L. Howard

Published in the United States by WaterBrook Multnomah, an imprint of the Crown Publishing Group, a division of Random House Inc., New York.

WATERBROOK and its deer colophon are registered trademarks of Random House Inc.

Library of Congress Cataloging-in-Publication Data
Weems, Stovall.
    Awakening : the 21-day experience that will revolutionize your relationship with God / Stovall Weems. — 1st ed.
        p. cm.
    Includes bibliographical references and index.
        ISBN 978-0-307-45953-4 (alk. paper) — ISBN 978-0-307-45954-1 (electronic : alk. paper)
    1. Spiritual life—Christianity. 2. Fasting—Religious aspects—Christianity. I. Title.
    BV4501.3.W4 2010
    248.4'7—dc22

                                                              2010042197

Printed in the United States of America
2013

10 9 8 7

SPECIAL SALES
Most WaterBrook Multnomah books are available at special quantity discounts when purchased in bulk by corporations, organizations, and special-interest groups. Custom imprinting or excerpting can also be done to fit special needs. For information, please e-mail SpecialMarkets@WaterBrook Multnomah.com or call 1-800-603-7051.

This book is dedicated to all our Celebration Church family.

I'm thankful for the privilege of being your pastor and love doing life with you guys. It's an honor to serve God with such an authentic, devoted, fired-up group of people.

CONTENTS

FOREWORD

I feel obligated to warn you. The author of this book, Stovall Weems, is not a normal person. You don't have to spend more than a few minutes with him to realize there is something different about this guy. His family is different. His church is different. His take on knowing and serving God is different.

You might say Stovall is a bit weird—in the best sort of way.

Let's face it. Normal is not working very well, is it? It's normal for marriages to end in divorce or limp along pathetically for years. It's normal for people to struggle financially, living paycheck to paycheck, hoping for a better day that never comes. It's normal for people to believe in God but live as if He doesn't exist. When it comes to most things in the world today—normal isn't working.

Thankfully, Stovall has written a book that is nothing close to normal.

When I first met Stovall several years ago, I realized we had similar stories. Although we are both pastors today, we weren't raised in Christian homes. In fact, we were both party guys. We both got into lots of trouble, chased lots of girls, and drank lots of cheap beer—and we both met the God we'd heard about in a very personal way. Because of God's love through His Son, Jesus, neither of us would ever be the same.

Overwhelmed with passion for this amazing God, both of us stepped into full-time vocational ministry. To be honest, when I became a pastor, I envisioned Bible studies, prayer meetings, and constant spiritual bliss. Instead I discovered that ministry is a real job and has real problems just like those every other person faces in this real world.

My once-raging fire for God started to cool. The light that had shone brightly for years quietly dimmed. My time in prayer became shorter and less meaningful. Before long, I read the Bible to prepare messages but not out of personal longing for God. I told scores of people that I'd pray for them, but I rarely did. I spoke the spiritual language but lacked real spiritual passion.

Spiritually, I started to fall asleep.

But one day, God clearly showed me something that jarred me awake: I'd become a full-time pastor and a part-time follower of Christ.

Perhaps you can relate. Maybe there was a time when you were closer to God than you are today. You loved His Word, craved His presence, and recognized His voice. God was everything to you. But life started happening. You didn't notice at first, but you started to slowly drift from Him. Weeks passed, then months, maybe even years. One day you realized that you'd been on a long spiritual nap. Now you're a full-time mom or businessperson or student or whatever—and a part-time follower of Christ.

If that's you—it's no accident you're holding this book in your hands. Like I said, Stovall is not a normal person. And this is not a normal book.

I can tell you honestly that Stovall's awakening message has impacted me personally in a life-altering way. When he first challenged me to seek God for twenty-one days, I was open to it—until he explained that we would be fasting. I quickly found several excuses to avoid anything that got between food and me. And my excuses held for two years straight.

However, after spending a weekend with Stovall at his church, God (through Stovall) convinced me to seek Him for an awakening—one that included fasting. Though it wasn't an easy journey, it was worth every sacrifice and more. Life, my church, my marriage, my family, and my passion for Christ have never been the same. I promise you that if you take this journey seriously, you'll see similar or even better spiritual results.

Open your heart. Open your mind. Open your spirit.

It's time for your awakening.

—CRAIG GROESCHEL
Senior Pastor, LifeChurch.tv
Edmond, Oklahoma

Awakening

Never be lacking in zeal, but keep your spiritual
fervor, serving the Lord.

—ROMANS 12:11, NIV

HOW CLOSE DO YOU FEEL TO GOD? Most of us sense that there's *more* to a relationship with God than what we currently are experiencing. But how do we develop a more intimate bond with Him?

As a devoted follower of Jesus, I have learned some secrets to staying consistently fresh in my relationship with God. This deepening friendship begins with what I call an *awakening*.

After an awakening, life is never the same.

A relationship with God is the most fulfilling thing a person can experience. Yet I have observed that while the vast majority of believers start out with a lot of passion and zeal in their relationship with God, over time that enthusiasm subsides.

On a day-to-day basis, their relationship with God eventually becomes passive. There are occasional bursts of excitement, but even that excitement is short-lived. Their walk with God seems to have a few highs, some lows...and a whole lot of mundane in-betweens.

> Passionate Christianity should be the norm for every believer—not the exception.

Why is that?

Does it strike you, as it has me, that there is something terribly wrong with that picture? Jesus said, "I have come that they may have life, and that they may have it more abundantly" (John 10:10). Aren't we vaguely unsettled with the idea that somehow a daily relationship with God...*the* God of the universe...can end up with the flavor of stale bread? The Bible is clear that our passion and "spiritual fervor" should be constant (Romans 12:11, NIV). So why have so many Christians accepted a faith experience that is so far below what God intended for them?

I believe we have an innate sense that serving and worshiping an infinitely powerful God should be anything but mundane. However, many people appear to think that dynamic interactions with God occur only at random times or, for some unknown reason, just are not happening now. And they certainly don't expect such encounters on a consistent basis. These believers find themselves at a loss as to how to recover the freshness and excitement they once felt and end up walking through life unaware that a passionate, thriving relationship with God should be the norm, not the exception, for every follower of Christ.

> We have an innate sense that serving and worshiping an infinitely powerful God should be anything but mundane.

Does any of this sound familiar to you? Maybe at one time you were excited about God, and were full of His life. Maybe you once felt free and were enjoying your relationship with God. But now, if you're honest, you know other things have grabbed your attention, and your heart has hardened to the joy and freshness you once felt. Or maybe you are far from God and struggling with addictive behavior or other issues. (And, by the way, is there really anyone who doesn't have issues?)

How is it that we can become content with a mediocre spiritual life? It's as if our soul itself grows dull and numb and needs to be shocked back to an awakened state. The good news is that the potential for a lasting, thriving relationship with God really is there. It just has to be awakened!

When I surrendered my life to Christ, one of the most powerful components of that experience was *awakening* to the very presence of God. I still remember the feeling. All of a sudden, my soul woke up. Deep inside, in an area I didn't even know existed, I felt new emotions and was so alive and full of joy, excitement, and freedom—all at the same time. This feeling was so good, so real, so authentic that I never wanted to lose it.

Since my awakening more than twenty years ago, I have been in a constant fight to keep that state of newness and freedom in my soul. And to this day nothing is as important to me as keeping my relationship with God fresh and new.

You may think that is an unrealistic, perhaps even undesirable, goal. After all, aren't new believers full of emotion and zeal? Eventually we have to calm down and get serious about following God, right? You may have even heard something like this a few times: "You can't always live on a mountaintop!" or, "You will be an emotional roller coaster if you base your walk with God on feelings."

On the contrary, this pursuit of "first love" or freshness has kept my spiritual walk consistent and thriving all these years. In how I relate to God and how I obey and trust Him, my heart has stayed in a posture of "want to" instead of "have to." Guarding the fire of devotion in my heart is the most foundational spiritual discipline of my Christian life. When that fire burns brightly, I love worshiping, praying, and obeying God. I hear His voice clearly, and my daily life is an overflow of power and grace. But when that fire dims and smolders, I find that even basic commitments become burdensome as I try to maintain them in my own strength.

> Guarding the fire of devotion in my heart is the most foundational spiritual discipline of my Christian life.

We can have now, on a daily basis, the same vital connection with Christ that we had on the day He saved us. "As you therefore have received Christ Jesus the Lord, so walk in Him" (Colossians 2:6). We are all called to be "zealous for good works" (Titus 2:14), and we're going to have to fight to "never be lacking in zeal" and always "keep [our] spiritual fervor" (Romans 12:11, NIV).

Maintaining this newness and freshness with God is something we must literally fight to protect. Make no mistake about it—we have a very real enemy who wants nothing more than for our souls to be lulled to sleep, all while we think everything's okay.

LIVE ON A MOUNTAINTOP?

So how do we continually experience newness in a world where everything ages? How do we experience freshness where everything quickly becomes stale? We have to wake up!

Awakening to the presence and power of God is both a one-time event and a recurring newness we experience throughout our lives. Some would say that this state of newness is a mountaintop experience, one that is nice to have every once in a while, but unsustainable in real life. But if you will stick with me, I will show you that not only is it possible to live a life fully awakened to God at all times, but it is the desire and will of God that you do so.

> Awakening to the presence and power of God is both a one-time event and a recurring newness we experience throughout our lives.

If we are not living that way, we have no one to blame but ourselves. If you don't believe me, then go ahead and put this book down and live how you want to live. But if you want an ongoing mountaintop experience, and if you're ready for your relationship with God to go to the next level, then keep reading and get ready for an incredible journey to your own personal awakening!

Your entire life really *can* be one big breakthrough. You *can* consistently feel God in your emotions and experience joy, even in the most difficult seasons of your life. That's what this book is about—I promise you that your immediate future can become the best time of your life! And this experience with God can be sustained year after year.

Don't allow the pain of this world to push you down into just biding your time here on earth and hoping for a better day in heaven. Yes, let's hope for a better day when we are all in heaven with Jesus, but until that time, let's live life as God intended it to be lived—fully awake, fully alive, and walking in a *continual* state of freshness and newness before God!

Regardless of where you find yourself today, you can live a life of passion for God. Remember, passionate Christianity is supposed to be the norm, not the exception. The principles of awakening to God and living a sustainable awakened lifestyle are the same principles that can get you free from addictions, bad habits, or anything else that is holding you back from God's best for your life.

I am not saying that every day will be like heaven on earth. I am not saying that you won't have days and seasons that feel drier than others—I have had my share of those. In my two-plus decades of walking with God I know

> Your entire life really can be one big breakthrough.

what it is to suffer, be disappointed, and feel discouraged. Neither am I saying that we should only live according to our feelings or base our relationship with God on experience alone.

I am saying I believe the Bible is clear about this: experiencing God and feelings go hand in hand. The Holy Spirit inside of us brings a whole new set of incredible emotions to life. God wants us consistently passionate for Him, and passion involves feelings!

Over the next chapters and in the "Awakening 21-Day Plan," I will show you how I keep things fresh and alive in my relationship with God. You, too, can apply these principles of spiritual renewal to your own life, and experience God's very best.

In this book I will tell you some of my story, walk you through a process of having your own personal awakening or reawakening with God, and show you how to keep that awakening experience vital, day after day and year after year. This book is about totally revolutionizing your walk with God so you can have the lasting, exciting relationship with Him you have dreamed about.

Awakening is an experience, but it must be based on a foundation of biblical truth and principles. There is no formula to this, but I believe there are progressive steps of understanding and decisions that if followed will lead almost everyone to a much deeper spiritual awareness and relationship with God. In the chapters that follow I will share what I call the steps of awakening. They are—

- experiencing surrender
- experiencing passion for God
- experiencing God's goodness
- creating space for God to fill

In a world where we're constantly bombarded with images, sounds, and counterfeit experiences that demand our attention and threaten to distract us, we can lose our spiritual focus and settle for cheap substitutes. We must discover how to remain awakened to God so that we can feel Him, hear Him, and have clear vision for our lives.

If you have lost your love, your passion, your "want to" attitude in your relationship with God, let's get those back. It is time to get your fight back, hit the reset button, and experience God in an incredibly fresh, new way.

Hold on and get ready for an awakening!

PART ONE

THE AWAKENING EXPERIENCE

2

Are You Awake?

CHRISTIANITY IS THE ONLY FAITH WHERE we are invited into a personal relationship with God. *The God of the universe.* And passionate spiritual zeal is one of the most important, evident qualities of having that personal relationship. The apostle Paul said, "Never be lacking in zeal, but keep your spiritual fervor, serving the Lord" (Romans 12:11, NIV).

But if most of us were honest, when it comes to how we view our relationship with God, the question in our hearts would be, *Never be lacking in zeal? Really? Is that even possible?* I would answer unequivocally, yes, it is. If God has commanded us to never lack in zeal, then He has also made a way for that to be possible.

> Passionate spiritual zeal is one of the most important, evident qualities of having a personal relationship with God.

Regardless of how long we have followed Jesus, the newness and zeal we experienced in Christ when we first received Him should continue to be evident in our everyday lives. If we're not experiencing that, then we need to ask ourselves why. Paul told his disciple Timothy "to fan into flames the spiritual gift God gave you" (2 Timothy 1:6, NLT). When the fire for God in our hearts begins to smolder, we must recognize that a key quality in our walk with God is missing.

THE DAY I WOKE UP

When my journey with Christ began, like many new believers, I really didn't know where to get started in living for God. I knew I was saved, I believed my sins were forgiven, and I was confident I was on my way to heaven. But what was next? I didn't know yet that I had only taken the first step.

If we really want to know God and experience Him, we have to go beyond the initial decision and come to a place of total surrender. After receiving Christ through salvation, the first step to a true awakening is to give it all up. Surrendering your life is more than just trusting in Jesus as your Savior so you can have forgiveness and go to heaven. It is not simply adding God to your life. To truly surrender means to get out of the pilot's seat and let Him take control. It means giving Him your whole life and discovering the reality, joy, peace, freedom, feelings, and experiences that come with truly knowing God. We often believe this is a one-time decision, but it is a practice we must regularly engage in to keep our spiritual fervor. Let me explain.

When I gave my life to Christ, I experienced some peace on the inside. I felt better because I knew I was saved, but I still didn't have the freedom I was looking for. I had made the decision, but I didn't have any real passion or power to live for God.

> We often believe surrender is a one-time decision, but it is a practice we must regularly engage in.

In the days that followed I would read the Bible, and that helped, but I just didn't get how it applied to my everyday life. I didn't know what a personal relationship with Jesus looked like or that God wanted me to live a life of freedom and power. And I certainly didn't know I could experience God in my emotions.

Because of all these factors, I went back and forth in my relationship with Jesus for about a year. I loved God, so I would do the Christian thing for a while. But then temptations would come and I would give in. Then I'd get back on track with God…then fall into temptation again…then live for God—you get the picture. While I never really returned to the lifestyle and destructive patterns I had before, I was inconsistent in my newfound faith. It was frustrating to say the least.

I finally came to a tipping point before the summer of my sophomore-junior-ish year. (I was on the six-year college plan at that point in my life!) One night, while at a Campus Crusade for Christ gathering, it suddenly hit me when the speaker said, "If you've never really walked with God, you need to walk with God this summer." At that instant I heard the Holy Spirit's voice in my heart say, *Stovall, you have never really walked with Me. You have never truly surrendered to Me.* I knew this meant that even though I had accepted Jesus, I had never completely surrendered my life to Him. I had simply added Him to my life so I could have relief, a better life, and a ticket to heaven. But I hadn't truly given Him every area to the point where I wanted to know Him and His will above all else.

Sadly, I think this is where a lot of Christians are today. While they have trusted in Christ for forgiveness and eternal life, they are still living life their own way and not really walking with God. A truly surrendered heart takes the next step and says about everything, "Have Your way, Lord."

This is when we start to experience the joy and presence of God to the fullest. When we are truly walking with God every day, it becomes the prayer of our hearts to continue doing so. In that moment at that campus meeting, the lights turned on for me. I knew I had heard the voice of God. Up to this point God had spoken to me through promptings, tugging on my heart, or thoughts inspired by the Holy Spirit. But this…this was different. This was a voice I heard deep inside of me, and with it I felt a rush of energy in my mind and heart. I knew that if I did not obey this voice, I would miss

> A truly surrendered heart says about everything, "Have Your way, Lord."

something important. I had been trying to know what God was really like for about a year and now this was my chance! God was giving me this incredible opportunity to know Him on a greater level, so it took me all of about a millisecond to declare in my heart, *Yes, God!*

I completely surrendered on the spot. No more adding God to my life because I wanted to go to heaven or because I knew that serving God was the right thing to do. No more going back and forth with one foot in the world and the other foot in God's kingdom. I finally understood that following Jesus was all or nothing. I knew God was saying to me, "Look, Stovall, if you want the life that I have for you, it begins with total surrender. If you want all of Me, then I need all of you."

In my heart as I responded, *Yes God!* I knew that meant completely leaving behind everything I had known, and that there would be real costs associated with the decision. But whether it was relationships, popularity, or whatever—I didn't care. I was ready to launch out into the deep. If Jesus was real and He was truth, there was really no other option.

Everything was different from that point on.

Through this step of total surrender, I was filled with the Holy Spirit and awakened to the very presence of God, and it was one of the most powerful experiences of my life. It was as if a big alarm clock had gone off inside me and my soul had awakened. Blinders fell off my eyes, and I began to see my whole life through a completely different filter. At last I tasted what true life was and should be like, and I could tell it was pure and authentic. It wasn't just powerful; it was personal. Through the presence of the Holy Spirit, God was now living inside me, and I could actually feel God in a concentrated form as His presence burned in my emotions.

For a guy like me, who had based his whole life on feeling good, this was just unbelievable. I had a new energy and enthusiasm about engaging God in worship, which became an outer expression of the love and thankfulness I felt for Him on the inside.

God's Word also became much more meaningful to me. Until this point, the Bible had not been that big a deal to me. In fact, when I would try to read, it would put me to sleep. But now the dots were connecting and I got it. And when I did, the Word started changing my life. It satisfied and strengthened me in a way that energized my whole being, and I found myself hungry for more.

That is exactly what happens when you awaken to God and "taste and see" that He is good (Psalm 34:8). Similar to our natural appetite for food, this supernatural hunger for God is awakened within you and drives you to pursue Him.

I'd finally found what I had been looking for, and I was never turning back.

AWAKENING IS FOR EVERYONE

It has been over twenty years now since I first truly awakened to an exciting, fresh, growing, personal relationship with God. My friendship with Him has changed and deepened over time, but it has been this lifestyle of pursuing that "first love" newness that has kept my spiritual walk consistent and thriving. I have "[fought] the good fight of faith" to guard my spiritual passion and experience the presence of God every day (1 Timothy 6:12).

Colossians 2:6 says, "As you therefore have received Christ Jesus the Lord, so walk in Him." I don't believe people have legitimate excuses for not experiencing the same spiritual passion today as on the first day they fell in love with Jesus. There is simply no substitute for a thriving, joyful, exciting life with God. Why would we ever desire anything less? I want my walk with God to stay fresh, and I want to enjoy my relationship with Jesus—and what I've discovered is that God wants this even more than I do.

Maybe you're reading this and realizing that you've never totally surrendered your life to God. Or maybe you did at one point have a fire that burned in your heart, but over time your heart has become lukewarm or hard, and you've lost your passion for God. Maybe you

> God will meet you right where you are.

love God, but the things of this world have bogged you down and you sense a need to surrender your life afresh to Him.

Whatever the case may be, I have some encouraging words for you: God will meet you right where you are. Any spiritual awakening always starts from a place of fresh surrender to God. And through our surrender, God fills us again with His presence through the power of the Holy Spirit. Ephesians 5:18 tells us to "be filled with the Spirit." That word filled means to always be full, not just to get filled one time. When we experience staleness in our relationship with God for whatever reason, surrendering again is the first step to rekindling the fire within.

James 4:10 says, "Humble yourselves before the Lord, and he will lift you up" (NIV). There's a whole new world waiting for you, but you must wake up. You can spiritually catch fire and move forward in your destiny with God. It's really the only way to live as a believer. But to get there, you've got to go all out. This means total surrender. No more halfway stuff! When you really experience the presence of God and the satisfaction He gives you on the inside, and when you believe that He wants you to experience that every day, you will *fight* to keep your spiritual fervor.

**This can and will be your best year ever,
if it is your best year spiritually.**

Even if you've given your life to God, even if you have known Him for a long time, I urge you to take this opportunity to surrender afresh. Ask God to show you any areas in your life you haven't completely given over to Him and surrender those to Him today.

You can either pray in your own words or use the prayer below as a guideline, but the key is to make sure this issue is settled in your heart before moving forward. May the cry of our hearts be, "Your will, not mine, Lord. Have Your way."

Dear Jesus, thank You for Your love, Your forgiveness, and Your goodness in my life. Lord, I humble myself before You, and I put all my trust and hope in who You are. I want to experience all that You have for me. I surrender my whole life to You. God, fill me with the Holy Spirit. Have Your way in my heart, and let my life glorify You. In Jesus' name, amen.

3

Passion and Authenticity

P ASSION IS THE ESSENCE OF AN AWAKENING experience. Passion in my relationship with God is the evidence of authentic affection for Him. From this place of passion is where I enjoy obeying God and feel that I am most glorifying to Him. God created us to be passionate about what we love; therefore, we should always be passionate for Him!

I was exposed to sports and athletics at a young age. Some of my earliest memories are of going to LSU football games with my dad. I was totally fascinated by the fan culture—which, if you've

> Passion in my relationship with God is the evidence of authentic affection for Him.

never experienced it, trust me, is a culture all its own. I remember feeling that incredible energy in the atmosphere. I could literally sense the passion, devotion, and commitment of those eighty thousand fans. Man, it was contagious!

I recently checked the dictionary definition of a *fan*. It simply means "an enthusiastic follower." This made me think about all the times throughout the Gospels that Jesus said, "Follow Me." I also thought about how the Bible says that we are to be enthusiastic in our relationship with God, for example, "Love the LORD your God with all your heart, with all your soul, with all your strength, and with all your mind" (Luke 10:27). That's enthusiasm! In fact, the word *enthusiasm* comes from two words, *en* and *theos,* meaning "in God." When you are in God, you will be energetic about it. A relationship with God goes hand in hand with passion.

In Jesus' day, they didn't use the term *fan.* If you followed a person or a movement then, you were simply called a *follower.* But I believe that when Jesus said, "Follow Me," He meant that He wanted true fans or enthusiastic followers. I think that believers today can get a great picture of what an enthusiastic follower of Jesus looks like by observing the characteristics of zealous sports fans.

There is one undeniable truth about true fans: *they are passionate.* Just watch any professional or college football game or any World Cup soccer match. As the cameras pan the crowd, you will see passion. The fans have pompoms. They're wearing the team colors. They have war paint on their faces. They are screaming. They may even be singing! They are just straight up into it. You may be such a fan of one or more sports teams yourself and go to the games. You know what it's like in the stadium—loud! The place rocks with passion, because real fans are passionate about their team.

As passionate followers of God, a church service should reflect some of the same excitement. Of course we all have our different personalities and styles, but when people come into the house of the living God, they should be able to sense and see the excitement of all of His fans! We're there to celebrate the God of the universe who loves us! People should be able to *feel* the life-giving presence of God that has the power to strengthen, refresh, and renew them. The atmosphere should feel authentic (not weird or spooky!) and be electric with contagious passion for Him.

> Being emotional about God is not removed or disconnected from good doctrine; it's affirmed in good doctrine.

Being emotional about God is not removed or disconnected from good doctrine; it's affirmed in good doctrine. Doctrine is very important as it ensures that we are grounded in truth. God's Word is our ultimate authority, and the church's teaching should reflect the glory, greatness, and goodness of God. But at the same time, preaching and teaching that are grounded in sound doctrine and glorify God will actually produce passionate followers of Christ. Bible-based teaching will involve experience and feeling, as well as knowledge and understanding.

PASSION IN WORSHIP

Here's another truth about fans: real fans are passionate about their teams' fight songs. I have personally experienced this many times when it comes to college football. The real fans are into it; they love to cheer and sing about their team. All they have to do is hear the first few notes and they jump to their feet and start singing passionately. True fans don't even have to be at a game! They can be out shopping or driving in the car, but if they hear the melody of that fight song, they instinctively want to belt out the words and get pumped up for the team.

Well, you know what? In the church, we have our own type of team fight songs; they're called praise songs. When we come into the house of God and hear the sounds of praise and worship, it's like Jesus is coming on the field. When we're passionate for God, we can't help but instantly engage in worship just like we instantly engage in our team's fight song. We are excited to encounter the living God in our worship, because the Bible says that God inhabits the praises of His people (Psalm 22:3, KJV). And how much more should we engage God? Before we're a Bulldog, or a Gator, or a Tiger, or a Yankee, or a Raider, or a Cowboy, we're followers of our risen Savior!

In order for our worship to be authentic, we must be passionate for God. Worship is an instinctive by-product of our thoughts and feelings about Him. When I went to football games as a boy, no one had to teach me how to cheer for the team by saying, "Stovall, let me instruct you here. It's okay to clap if the team makes a good play, and you can shout and get excited. And this may really surprise you, but you can raise your hands if your team scores a touchdown!"

Today, I can assure you that at any football, soccer, basketball, or baseball game, the real fans will be lifting their hands, clapping, and jumping up and down. They're going to be high-fiving one another. Why? Because real fans express genuine, authentic passion for their team. Likewise, real followers of Christ will express genuine, authentic passion toward Him. But remember, "God is Spirit, and those who worship Him must worship in spirit and truth" (John 4:24). That means it's not an outward show of cheering and waving of arms that ultimately matters to God. He wants sincere devotion in our hearts.

PASSION EXPRESSES EMOTION

God created us to be passionate about what we love. If we love something (or someone), we can't keep quiet about it. We easily express our feelings and emotions. Our actions show that our relationship and affection toward that person, thing, team, or hobby are authentic. I have never met a person who was not at least somewhat emotional about what he was passionate about. This is a basic trait of human nature.

The same principle applies in how we relate to God. He created us in His image with emotions so that we could feel and express His love in our hearts, souls, and strengths, not just our minds. Our souls and our strengths speak specifically of our emotions and physical bodies. *Genuine spiritual passion comes from our hearts, but it manifests itself in our emotions and lifestyles.* When you have an awakening experience with Jesus and have the Holy Spirit living inside you, there's no way you won't express passion for the One you love!

> God created us to be passionate about what we love.

You might want to say, "Stovall, that stuff's too emotional for me."

My answer to that: I promise you that whatever you are passionate about, you will also be emotional about. Passion involves emotion.

I know that emotion is expressed differently by different types of people. But my point is that true followers of Jesus are enthusiastic (not weird or obnoxious!) followers. *Our enthusiasm is a key part of our witness to others.* It is the evidence that our relationship with Jesus is authentic. This is one of the main reasons Jesus sent the Holy Spirit and why the first of the nine fruits of the Spirit is love (Galatians 5:22). Love is felt in our emotions and is a prompting force. When we are filled with the love of Christ, when "the love of Christ compels us" (2 Corinthians 5:14), we are emotionally driven to express gratitude and affection to God.

If you go further down the list, the next two fruits of the Spirit are "joy" and "peace" (Galatians 5:22). Once again, those are attitudes and states of mind that you can feel and experience.

God shows us very clearly throughout His Word that we should be experiencing certain feelings as part of our faith. The Bible says that "the kingdom of God is…righteousness and peace and joy" (Romans 14:17). The kingdom of God is wherever the rule and reign of Jesus Christ is established. So when you surrendered your life to Christ, His rule and reign covered your life and you were "made right with God" (Romans 10:4, NLT)—and peace and joy are an indispensable part of our right standing with God.

This is why the Bible says not only to "serve the LORD" but also to do so "with gladness" (Psalm 100:2). We are commanded not just to give but also to be "a cheerful giver" (2 Corinthians 9:7). The Bible doesn't say just to pray but also to pray fervently (James 5:16). It says, "The joy of the LORD is [our] strength" (Nehemiah 8:10), and, "Happy are the people whose God is the LORD" (Psalm 144:15).

> Whatever you are passionate about, you will also be emotional about.

Do you see what I'm saying? These are Christlike attitudes that come with feelings. They are intertwined with our faith. When our feelings don't line up with what God's Word says we should be feeling, we need to ask ourselves why. He still loves us the same and relates to us through His goodness and mercy, but He wants us to consistently feel His peace, joy, and gladness in our emotions. That way we can enjoy our lives and glorify Him as well as have the strength to serve Him.

Why wouldn't people want to feel and experience more of God in their everyday lives? I believe they do, but they don't expect this to happen on a regular basis because they believe that such feelings and encounters with God are just for now and then.

Whether it is marriage, family, sports teams, or hobbies—passion is evidence of that authenticity. In love there is a strong component of faithfulness and commitment that goes beyond feelings, but true love— the kind we all want to receive and the kind that we practice when we are at our best—comes with feelings. And our love for God is really no different.

> When our feelings don't line up with what God's Word says we should be feeling, we need to ask ourselves why.

When others see the authenticity of our passion for God, it will make a distinct impression and be a witness to them. Do you realize that the evidence of passion for God in our lives can actually point people to Jesus? If you are passionate about sports or hobbies, that's awesome; but let's make sure our passion for God exceeds every other passion in our lives, because passion for God makes a difference in advancing the kingdom of heaven. When you're passionate about Jesus—in other words, a true fan, an enthusiastic follower— it's always a win. In fact, it's a blowout win every time!

Let's review the key steps so far in the process of awakening:

- experiencing surrender
- experiencing passion for God

After what I've presented in this chapter, I hope you can see that passion is a significant part of our relationship with God. God wants us consistently passionate for Him. In this book I'm going to show you how to get the fire of God burning in your heart and how to keep it. This is what the awakening lifestyle is all about. If you are still struggling to understand how this could become true in your life, ask God to help you. Remember, He wants this more than you do.

An Awakening Story

Throughout the book I will present stories of people who have experienced increased intimacy with God and the release of His grace and power through an awakening experience.

Filling a God-sized Hole in My Heart

I grew up in a traditional church where the power of the Holy Spirit did not seem living and active. Church life was average at best, and the thought of living a life as a Christian just seemed flat-out boring. I turned away from God for about ten years during high school and college; however, I always kept Him in my back pocket in case I found myself desperate and in need of help. I drifted far from God while I sought fulfillment from chasing all the wrong things: women, material objects, and the wrong idea of success.

In my midtwenties, I found out about Celebration Church through some friends. The music, the atmosphere, and the power of the worship at Celebration were unlike anything I had ever experienced as a child. Most importantly, I found myself surrounded by Christians who were living and modeling an authentic life for Christ. These people were different. They were passionate. Jesus Christ was not just a figure to them; He was alive. Christ was a friend.

Within months of my first visit to Celebration Church, I experienced a rock bottom and realized that the lack of fulfillment in my life was a God-sized hole in my heart and I was determined to get it filled.

In January 2008, Celebration was on a churchwide twenty-one-day season of prayer and fasting. I did not personally participate in the *entire* twenty-one days of the fast that year, but I would have to say that the spiritual momentum the church gained through the fast overflowed out to me. I recognized for the first time that *this* is what my relationship with God was supposed to be like: passionate.

I took the step to fully surrender my life to Christ. From that moment, God poured His grace and love all over me. Awakening to Him was exactly what I needed in my life. I finally felt free and empowered to carry out God's greater plan for my life as a passionate Christ-follower. I am confident in who I am in Christ, and He has really shifted my focus to where I am less concerned about myself and more concerned about others.

Since then, I've gotten married, and my relationship with my wife is one that is grounded on these truths as well. God's love is actively working not only in me but now through me as well. I now serve at the church, frequently go on mission trips, and love giving of my time to serve others. It's awesome and incredibly rewarding knowing that I'm a part of moving His kingdom forward.

—JONATHAN BAJALIA

4

Rediscover Grace

S PIRITUAL DISCIPLINES SUCH AS FASTING, prayer, and studying God's Word are key components to the awakening lifestyle. They can fuel our passion for God, and in the following chapters we will be discovering them in a fresh way. But to enjoy those benefits long term we must first make sure we have the proper mind-set for how we view them. Bible reading, fasting, prayer, and, in fact, all methods of drawing closer to God must be seen through the filter of the goodness and greatness of God.

In our modern culture, and even in Christian circles at times, the word *grace* has lost its power and become commonplace. We use the word for everything. We give grace, we say grace, and we name our baby girls Grace. We say that people have grace. We have grace periods on our credit card payments. Grace. Grace. Grace.

> All methods of drawing closer to God must be seen through the filter of the goodness and greatness of God.

Grace is also commonly associated with words like *nice, merciful,* or *loving,* but it is so much more powerful than that. Grace is the very foundation of our walk with God. This might seem a little basic to you, but trust me, it's crucial that we revisit the foundational work of grace.

I like to put it this way: "The grace of God is the practical working of the goodness of God in the life of the believer." How does that change the way you relate to God? The truth is, even though we understand the freedom grace brings, we have more of a tendency to relate to God based on our evaluation of ourselves. But God wants our relationship with Him to be based on how He views us, and He views us through the completed work of His Son. When we trust and rest in the completed work of Christ, we walk in grace. Let's consider some examples.

LAYING THE PROPER FOUNDATION

Two of the greatest enemies to our faith are condemnation and a lack of understanding the Word of God. Either we don't know the Word of God or we don't truly understand it. As a result we don't recognize who we are in Christ. God said, "My people are destroyed for lack of knowledge" (Hosea 4:6). If we don't have the proper knowledge of the power of grace, we will be severely hindered in achieving our potential as mature followers of Jesus.

Then there is condemnation. It may surprise you, but do you know that if you love God and you want to please Him, you are a great target for condemnation? This is because even though we want to please God, we are human and will never perfectly obey Him in all areas of our lives all the time. We have weaknesses and we succumb to temptation sometimes. We make mistakes, or we sin, and then the enemy accuses us and we feel condemned. *If you aren't firmly grounded in an understanding of grace and the New Covenant, guilt and shame will take the joy—and therefore the strength—from your relationship with God.*

> If we don't have the proper knowledge of the power of grace, we will be severely hindered in achieving our potential as mature followers of Jesus.

When it comes to personal devotional times, fasting, and prayer, it is easy to slip into a legalistic mentality. We can begin to think that God is more pleased with us because of our self-denial and discipline, when in fact there's no amount of self-denial that could lift us up enough to satisfy the standards of a holy God. Only Jesus could satisfy those standards.

In a focused time of prayer and fasting, we sense or experience the pleasure, power, and presence of God to a greater degree. It's because we have taken the time and effort to draw near to Him. We are more spiritually sensitive, so we feel God more. We can hear His voice more clearly because we've shut out some of the day-to-day noise in our lives. God's power and presence are continually available to us in this way. Thanks to the blood of Jesus, God is always pleased with us. He constantly wants to speak to us. If we aren't enjoying the full benefits of the relationship, it's because we aren't tuned in to Him.

Having an unclear view of the New Covenant of grace can result in these types of faulty thinking patterns, which tends to happen if we have trouble connecting the content of the Old and New Testaments. Of course both testaments are the inerrant Word of God, but the Old Testament contains the Old Covenant, which was the system of the Law. The New Testament contains the New Covenant of grace, which came through Jesus. We now live under the New Covenant, so whenever we look at the Old Covenant of the Law, we must ensure we are seeing it through the filter of grace.

Some people think that when God conveyed the Law through Moses, His primary purpose was to show us the holy nature of God. This is not true. While the Law does reflect some of the moral attributes of God's character, God is infinitely more loving and holy than the Law. If we want to truly see God's nature, we must look at Jesus (John 14:9).

> The primary intent of the Law was not to show us the holy nature of God. If we want to see God's nature, we must look at Jesus.

The purpose of the law was to keep Israel "under guard" (Galatians 3:23) so they wouldn't destroy themselves like many of the lawless societies and cultures of their day. The Law was also given to reveal the fallen nature of mankind, to help us recognize how desperately we needed a Savior.

Because God is loving and just, and because we are not, it was evident that we would never be able to earn our way to a satisfying relationship with Him. No matter how hard we might try in our own strength, because of our sinful nature not one of us could ever fulfill the requirements of the Law perfectly and work our way to God. We would always fall short of His glorious standard (Romans 3:23).

Another purpose of the Law was to show us that sin destroys people, and sin must be punished. If God did not punish sin, He would not be morally consistent and just. Sin messes everything up for people. Therefore, God wants to eradicate sin and its effects, somewhat as a good doctor seeks to eradicate an infection like pneumonia with antibiotics. God is a benevolent Creator and the eternal harmony of the universe is dependent on His ruling with justice.

God needed to show us that there would be consequences for sin and that we would miss the mark every time. God used the Law to show us that we need help! In order for us to have a lasting, secure relationship with God and to escape eternal judgment for our sins, there had to be a solution. And it had to be a permanent solution.

The answer is the grace found through the New Covenant. God established a way through Jesus Christ. Let's look at the main clause of the New Covenant in Hebrews 8:10–12:

This is the covenant that I will make with the house of Israel after those days, says the LORD: I will put my laws in their mind and write them on their hearts; and I will be their God, and they shall be My people. None of them shall teach his neighbor, and none his brother, saying, "Know the LORD," for all shall know Me, from the least of them to the greatest of them. For I will be merciful to their unrighteousness, and their sins and their lawless deeds I will remember no more.

Wow! That's just awesome.

In this passage God described the New Covenant He was to make with believers. The New Covenant was all about creating a way for us to have a personal relationship with God based solely on His goodness. The plan was for a relationship in which we could be declared righteous based not on our behavior but on God's love for us. A relationship where we could stand perfected before God, not because of what we do or don't do, but because of His goodness through Christ. His plan was to deal with the sin that separated us from Him, once and for all. God did this by *forgiving* our sins. Not by pretending they don't exist, and not by winking at them and giving us a free pass because He loves us. If He were to just wink at our sin and let it slide, He wouldn't be God. Remember, sin offends Him and He's perfectly just. God did something much more powerful than give us a free ride. He called into remembrance all of our sins—at one time. How did He do that?

God is in eternity. He looks at time from a bird's-eye view. He identified every sin that you and I and everyone who's ever lived or will live will commit from the time of birth to death. God called all these sins into remembrance. He executed His full wrath, His full punishment, His full displeasure, His full disappointment, His full judgment, and His full condemnation for these sins on His own Son. Only someone as righteous and holy as Jesus could stand in the gap for us, and He did it obediently.

The Bible says that when Jesus came to earth, He fulfilled the Old Covenant of the Law in that He obeyed God perfectly in every motive, thought, and ac-

> "Our old man was crucified with Him, that the body of sin might be done away with, that we should no longer be slaves of sin."

tion (1 Peter 2:22). He met the standard we could never meet. He lived a completely innocent life, not deserving any punishment and certainly not death, yet He chose to offer His life as the sacrifice for our sins, paying the debt we could never pay.

Sin and its effects were completely eradicated through the blood of Christ. This is why the Bible says that now God remembers our sins no more (Hebrews 8:12). They are gone—eradicated forever by the work of Christ (Romans 6:6). All of your past, present, and future sins have been totally forgiven, done away with forever!

This is why the Bible says, "As He is, so are we in this world" (1 John 4:17). Consider the relationship between God the Father and Jesus. Is the Father displeased with Jesus in any way? No! Does Jesus have the power and favor of God? Absolutely, yes! And, therefore, so do you and I. Because as He is, so we are. Ephesians 2:6 says that we are seated in the heavenly places in Christ Jesus. He completely saved us to the uttermost (Hebrews 7:25), and that's where we are in Christ. Case closed. Now that's really good news!

Grace is the undeserved favor of God. Grace is God equipping you free of charge to be who He's called you to be. Grace is the understanding that everything we have in Christ is based entirely on the goodness of God and His love for us. I could go on and on. I could walk you through Romans and

> Our entire relationship with God and the power that comes with it will only be experienced if you believe and rest in the goodness of God.

Hebrews and Ephesians and basically all of the New Testament and show you that our entire relationship with God and the power that comes with it will only be experienced if you believe and rest in the goodness of God. Stop focusing on your faults and focus on His goodness.

The gospel means "the good news." God is in love with you and God really is that good—even better than you could imagine.

THE TRAP OF PERFORMANCE

The problem is that we have a hard time believing that grace is true. And of course the king of all liars—Satan—works nonstop to convince us that *God* is the One not telling the truth! Many believers today still have what I call a law-based or Old Covenant–style relationship with God. Their relationship with Him is rule-based or legalistic. This type of relationship flows out of a belief system that basically says, "If I do good, if I perform well today, God's going to be pleased with me. God's going to like me, and God's going to bless me. And if I don't perform well today, God's not going to like me. He's not going to bless me and be pleased with me." That thinking is so far from the truth! But since this is how the world we live in operates, it's easy to fall for the lie.

Can you see how that mind-set leads to a performance-based belief system not much different than the Law? Due to our human nature, we will never hit the mark 100 percent of the time. *When we relate to God based on how we perform, we are unwittingly working contrary to the necessary sacrifice of Jesus.* To live in the freedom that Jesus died to give us, we absolutely must focus on the goodness of God.

Too many people, though, come to church and instead of encountering God and His truth, they encounter religion and rules. They bump into a system that says, "You need to clean up your act—or else." Instead of accepting people for who they are and where they are, and allowing the goodness and grace of God to transform them from the inside out, many churches place an emphasis on conformity and transformation from the outside in. That's why legalistic people don't like too much teaching on the goodness of God. In fact, they think too much teaching on the goodness of God will encourage people to

> Too many people come to church and instead of encountering God and His truth, they encounter religion and rules.

sin more. I contend it will do just the opposite. Teaching on the goodness of God will make people want to sin less because it is "the goodness of God [that] leads you to repentance" (Romans 2:4). The power of grace comes to us when we have a revelation of the goodness of God, and without grace we cannot overcome sin (Romans 6:14). The Bible says that "we love Him because He first loved us" (1 John 4:19). The way we love God more is by focusing on His love for us. You will live more holy on accident by focusing on the goodness of God than you will by focusing on all the "thou shalts" and the "thou shalt nots."

This also has a direct correlation with our feelings. Our feelings result from whatever we are focused on. That's why it's so important to focus on the goodness of God through His Word. Right thinking leads to right feeling, and the way we think right is to renew our minds in the Word of God.

When we understand who we are in Christ, we experience His peace, joy, and gladness. However, focusing on our faults will actually have the opposite result, and we'll end up feeling condemned. God doesn't love us any less, but we are not experiencing His best.

When I first became a Christian, I was fully walking in a grace relationship with God, because I knew there was absolutely nothing I did to earn my salvation. I knew how absolutely sinful my life had been. I was doing so much wrong and my lifestyle was so far from God that when I received Jesus, I knew beyond a shadow of a doubt that it was all because of the goodness of God and none of my own!

> Many people think focusing on the goodness of God will encourage people to sin more. I contend it will do just the opposite.

God forgave all of my sins and I was fired up! I was full of life and walking in faith—it was awesome. Of course I made mistakes and fell short because of ignorance. But I had done so much bad the previous twenty years of my life, I knew that if God forgave me for all of those sins, then He could forgive me for all my new ones. My failures didn't have any condemnatory power, because I knew God had saved me—not because of how I performed, but because of His goodness.

That's where God wants us to stay for all of our Christian life! Colossians 2:6 says, "As you therefore have received Christ Jesus the Lord, so walk in

Him." You received Jesus not through the merits of your own performance, but through grace. Your walk with God should continue in that same way, all the days of your life.

When I first started walking with God, I totally related to Him through a filter of grace. I didn't know any other way. At some point early on, though, I connected into a group of people who were...well, the only way to describe them was they were really strict and set themselves apart from other believers in terms of the discipline of their lifestyle. They began to challenge me and question my church and imply that I had a lesser revelation of God's holiness. The main ministry of these people seemed to be that of rebuking, judging, and preaching on judgment and their version of holiness. They believed that pretty much the entire body of Christ was backslidden and that in order for me to really please God, I should embrace their view and join their separatist doctrine.

As a brand-new believer, this was all very attractive to me because I wanted to please God so much. I didn't know it until later but these folks weren't more holy; they were just harsh. Harshness isn't holiness, but it is easy to confuse the two, and that's just what I did.

Looking back, I would say that this group wasn't a cult; they were just legalistic, and had no grounding in the love and goodness of God. Before long, my relationship with God, which had started full of life and innocence, turned into this performance-driven, legalistic way of living. I tried to please God every day, but if I didn't perform right, I truly believed He was displeased with me.

I tried to log a certain number of hours a day in prayer and Bible reading. In fact, I used to pray from five

> Harshness isn't holiness, but it is easy to confuse the two.

to seven in the morning five days a week because I heard a famous preacher say that unless you pray two hours a day, God will probably pass over you and not be able to use you. I also spent a certain amount of time each week fasting and witnessing. I became an expert in legalism.

It got so bad at one point that if one of my friends tried to talk to me before I was done with my two hours of prayer, I'd just look at him, hold up my watch, and point to the dial, all the while continuing to pray right in his face. Oh yeah, I was a psycho!

Why did I practice such a hardcore lifestyle of legalism? Because I so wanted to please God and since I was not properly grounded in the grace of God, I fell right into this trap.

At that stage of my life, I was extremely sin conscious and trying so hard to do the right thing. Yet it was probably the most ineffective season in my entire ministry. My ability to effectively share Christ with others was at its weakest, and I probably demonstrated less Christlikeness than ever before or since. It was all born out of a sincere desire to please God, but legalism can only produce one of two things in your life, and neither of them is good.

First of all, if you perform well, guess what that leads to? *Pride.* On the other hand, if you don't perform well, the fruit is *condemnation.* Either way the fruit of having a performance-based relationship is a lose-lose situation. If we try to come to God based on our performance, guess what? It will never be good enough. None of us could ever be that good; only Jesus was able to do that. Do you see what I'm saying? That's why we have to focus on God's love for us.

START YOUR DAY WITH THE RIGHT MIND-SET

Having the right kind of mind-set requires intentionality. We have to be aware that our natural, human instinct when we wake up each day will be to gravitate toward everything we think is wrong in our lives. So we have to be intentional about setting our focus with the right perspective before we start moving forward with our day.

I want to share with you how I do this. For quite some time now, I have practiced this in my daily devotions and it has changed the way I view each day. I do this not only when things are going well, but on the tough days too.

Every day as I direct my attention to God in a concentrated way, the first thing I do is make sure I focus on the goodness, greatness, and glory of God. Focusing daily on these three attributes of God gives me a complete picture or filter of His grace. My model for this is the first line of the Lord's Prayer in Matthew 6:9. I've also noticed that nearly every prayer the apostle Paul prayed for the New Testament churches follows this same pattern as well.

The Lord's Prayer starts with "Our Father." You have to remind yourself that you are a child of God and that all your sins are forgiven (John 1:12; 1 John 2:2). You have to know that you are going to heaven and have eternal life through Jesus (Romans 5:21). You have to know that you have the favor of God and that God is for you (Romans 8:31). You need to remind yourself every day that your real home is not here on earth but in heaven (1 John 2:17). Your life on earth is so temporary, but your life with your heavenly Father is forever (Colossians 3:1–3). Thank God for who He is and for all He has done for you.

But it doesn't stop there. You might be thinking, *Well, that's great, Stovall, I know God loves me, and that He's for me, but that doesn't make the daily challenges in my life go away. I'm still facing some serious difficulties.* You're absolutely right. That's why after we focus on the goodness of God, we must then focus on the *greatness* of God.

The next two words in the Lord's Prayer are "in heaven." Heaven speaks to the greatness of God and the greatness of His power within all who believe in Him. We have to remember that God is on the throne, and with Him "all things are possible" (Mark 10:27). Jesus has all authority (Matthew 28:18), and as a child of God, all the power of heaven is at your disposal. The same power that raised Jesus from the dead lives within you (Romans 8:11). With Jesus inside you, you can face anything! You can have faith that will move mountains if you will only believe (Matthew 17:20). So believe in God for the supernatural and know that He will work all things in accordance with His will (Romans 8:28). Bring all your cares, problems, trials, and pain to the Lord and believe Him for great things (1 Peter 5:7). Believe in your heart, "I can do all things through Christ who strengthens me" (Philippians 4:13).

Remember, God says He gives us peace and joy in believing, not in achieving. No matter what you are going through, trust God and you can experience His joy and peace. He gives that to us as we trust in Him. Most people think that the only joy is when the prayer is answered or their circumstance is changed. Not true—it's every day as you walk with God. That's awakening!

The final thing we focus on is the glory of God: "Hallowed be Your name." This helps us remember that this life is not all about us. Hallowed means "sanctified" or "lifted up"; in other words, "Glorified be the name of God." Our lives on this earth are but a speck in the big picture of eternity. They're like a vapor. Yet so many times we focus on our comforts and preferences when those things are really not going to make a bit of difference in the big picture. Keeping an eternal perspective helps us remember that if we have to go through something we would prefer to not go through, we can still enjoy our relationship with God.

My number one priority every day is to live for the glory of God regardless of what comes my way. I choose to be content with where God has me for this season and glorify Him regardless of what my personal preferences are (Philippians 4:12).

When you get up in the morning, your number one priority should be to get in the right mind-set for your day. Focus first on what's right about God, and see everything else through that filter. Remember, it's not about what you do. It's about who God is.

> It's not about what you do. It's about who God is.

The only way you're going to consistently enjoy your relationship with God, the only way you're going to really have this incredible supernatural life full of peace and joy, is not if you obey God perfectly, but if you truly believe and focus on how much He loves you. When you walk with God and focus on His love for you, that is called walking in the grace of God.

Let's get the right mind-set so we don't become prideful or condemned.

When we get on fire for God and experience our awakening, our passion for God needs to be consistent and constant, and the only constant is the grace of God found in Jesus and His love for us.

This is where we are on our path to an awakening:

- experiencing surrender
- experiencing passion for God
- experiencing God's goodness

The best news we could ever receive is that God relates to us based on the finished work of Christ. That's the difference maker. That's the constant in the awakening lifestyle. That's good news we can celebrate—every day!

An Awakening Story

A Breakthrough to Freedom

Before the awakening fast began, I actually found myself thinking far too much about what the right fast was. I fumbled through all the different options, worried that if I didn't do it correctly I would sabotage God's plans. While I desperately wanted a new thing to take place in my relationship with God, the same confusion and fear that had hobbled me for so long dominated my attempts to find an answer.

As I realized that I was lost in trying to rationalize the process of fasting, I finally stopped thinking about these things and instead began to seek God in prayer about what I should do. He led me to my answer, which was to begin by writing down those things that compelled me to fast. I knew that my reasons were not only to draw closer to God but to break up the cold and fallow ground of my heart in the process. I also knew I needed to recognize a deeper dependence on Him.

I then felt God prompting me to move forward with the fast, committing these things to Him in prayer each day and then asking the Holy Spirit what I should eat, meal by meal. I struggled with this instruction, as I am far too aware of how fraught with potential self-deception this could be and would have been way more comfortable with a traditional, normal fast. Nonetheless, I started my fast this way, believing that if I went at it with the right heart, I wouldn't miss the mark.

Through this process of letting go, I discovered the goodness of God in such a powerful way. I learned to recognize His voice more distinctly and rely on it to guide me. This fast also started to chop away at the source of my warped view of God and myself, a view that was grounded in a legalistic, man-made religion.

Through the fast, I grew so much closer to Him and saw how very good He is and how much goodwill He really has toward me. He tore right at the root of all that had held me back for so long, and I was finally able to enjoy the freedom of living completely reliant on Him.

That daily process of devotion has continued well past the twenty-one days. It has become an essential part of my life, and through it an awesome transformation has occurred. I am now sixty pounds lighter and telling anybody who will listen the reason why. What they see on the outside is just a reflection of an even greater thing that has taken place within me.

The outward change has opened many doors to share about the inward change that makes it all possible. God is so rockin' awesome!

— KELLY WAGONER

5

God Is a Filler, Not a Forcer

THE PRINCIPLES WE'VE UNPACKED SO FAR are setting the stage for some incredible things to happen in your life. As you've read, I hope your faith has enlarged with each truth and you're recognizing how exciting and satisfying your daily relationship with God is intended to be.

Now that we have the proper foundation and the right mind-set in place, we're ready to discover (or rediscover) the concepts of personal devotion, prayer, and fasting. This begins by recognizing that in life, when we want something new and exciting to happen, we have to create some space.

Take, for example, expecting a first child. One of the most exciting things for soon-to-be parents is creating the space in their home for a nursery. Expectant moms are celebrated with baby showers, and they enjoy selecting and decorating with the perfect colors, patterns, and furniture. Eager dads, especially those expecting a boy, will go through tremendous effort to find all their favorite sports team paraphernalia and then pick the perfect spot in the nursery to showcase it.

While that whole process is fun and exciting, it's really not this new room that excites us the most. It's more the anticipation and joy we have about the baby who will fill that room. The whole point of *creating* the space is *filling* the space, and because of that, the space has special significance.

I want you to consider this idea from a spiritual perspective. Think about an area of your life where you want God to do something new. Or maybe you're hoping for His strength and guidance with a certain problem you are facing. You know that God's nature is to create new things and that He has the answers you need to endure life's challenges. But let me ask, have you created the space in your life for God to fill? For as much as God wants to do something amazing in your life, He is a filler, not a forcer.

Here's another sports analogy to illustrate my point: When a football team has a gifted athlete in its lineup, the coaches will design specific plays for this player. For example, the athlete may be so talented the coaches don't need to tell him, "Go to this hole," or, "Cut this way." This guy's so good that he will instinctively see the hole. The rest of the team simply has to create the space where he can make something happen. These are space-making plays. The coach knows that if he can just get the athlete into the open space, a big play is possible.

> When we want something new and exciting to happen, we have to create some space.

Something similar should occur in our relationship with God. Too often we spend so much time and energy trying to figure everything out and anticipate every scenario. We want God to do this; we want God to do that. But all the while God is saying, "Just create a little space for Me, and I'll come in and fill it."

God is so loving…merciful…powerful. His ways are "higher than [our] ways" (Isaiah 55:9). He knows what we really need. We just have to create the space.

THREE SPACE-MAKERS

Jesus showed us three ways to create a space in our lives for God to fill. When He talked about each one of these, He gave them a name. Here's what He said:

> When you do a charitable deed, do not let your left hand know
> what your right hand is doing, that your charitable deed may be in

secret; and your Father who sees in secret will Himself reward you openly.... When you pray, go into your room, and when you have shut your door, pray to your Father who is in the secret place; and your Father who sees in secret will reward you openly.... But you, when you fast, anoint your head and wash your face, so that you do not appear to men to be fasting, but to your Father who is in the secret place. (Matthew 6:3–4, 6, 17–18)

Notice that Jesus first talked about giving, then prayer, and, finally, fasting. Jesus didn't say "if" you do these things. He said "when" you do them. He assumed that, as His children, we would want to create spaces in our lives for Him to fill with His rewards.

Notice that He also referred to each created space as "the secret place." The word *secret* in the Greek actually means "covered, hidden, set apart." And *place* does not refer to just an average place. It actually means the highest or upper place. This is the same wording used to describe an "upper room." It is a higher, covered, special place where you and God meet.

I find this very interesting: When God wanted to fill believers with the Holy Spirit, the most amazing filling of all, He didn't ask them to think it all through and figure out how that was going to happen. He also didn't force it upon them. He revealed what was in store for them and asked them to be ready, but then He asked them to create a space where it could happen (Acts 1:4).

It's the same thing with us spiritually. As we anticipate God bringing power and blessing into our lives, we must be intentional about creating space for it to occur—when we give, when we pray, and when we fast. When we create these spaces, we will have an upper-room type of experience. Don't try to figure everything out. Just create some space for God.

> Don't try to figure everything out. Just create some space for God.

Remember, God is a filler, not a forcer.

WHEN YOU GIVE

When you give to God, you create a space for Him to move in your finances. Part of the purpose for tithing is to give God space to adjust your financial situation. If you give God 10 percent of your earnings, you have created a 10 percent hole or space in your financial portfolio. You might think, *Well, that's not all that much.* But when God fills, He also multiplies. Remember the story of the boy who had the two fish and five loaves of bread? Jesus multiplied what he gave and it fed five thousand families! They even had leftovers to spare (John 6:1–14). When you give to God and create space, He makes what you have left go even further.

There are also times when God may ask you to give a special offering above and beyond your tithe. When He does that, He's inviting you to create some special space. Don't try to figure it all out. Remember, God's ways are much higher than our ways. You will bless others and may witness a financial miracle!

If you want to experience a move of God in your finances, create the space. Remember, God is a filler, not a forcer. You do what you can, and God will show up in ways that blow your mind!

WHEN YOU PRAY

One morning during our most recent twenty-one-day fast, I was in my room having my personal devotion time. My ten-year-old son, Stovie, was also in his room doing his Awakening kid's devotional for that day. All of a sudden, Stovie burst into my room and said, "Dad! Dad! I was doing my devotional in my room like you're doing right now, and then I got to the prayer part and started praying to God." He could hardly get the words out, he was talking so fast. "All of a sudden, on the inside of me, I felt this warmth and, like, this fire, deep down on the inside of me. Dad, is that God? Is that God, Dad?"

You can imagine what kind of "dad moment" that was for me. I could see it written all over his face. He had just experienced the tangible presence of God. He was enjoying an awakening.

"Yes! Yes it is, Stovie," I said. "God is always there, on the inside of you, even when you don't feel Him. But because you're now going to God in your personal devotion time and in prayer, you've created a space for Him to fill. And you're starting to feel the evidence of His presence on the inside of you. That's what happens when you create space for God."

Stovie's face lit up and he was fired up for the rest of the day. His confidence went through the roof, and he beamed with excitement.

Ephesians 3:20 says, "Now to Him who is able to do exceedingly abundantly above all that we ask or think. . ." Way beyond what we *think* we need, God *knows* what we need. He knows exactly what will strengthen and encourage us. We simply have to create the space for Him to fill. That's what prayer does.

WHEN YOU FAST

Fasting is another way we make space for God to fill. I have been fasting regularly for over twenty years now, and each time I do, I experience God in a powerful—often surprising—way.

During Awakening 2010 at our church, God spoke to me about extending my usual twenty-one-day fast to forty days. I was forty years old, and I felt that 2010 would be a significant year for me. So I planned out my fast and started it with the rest of our church.

About halfway through the forty days I flew to Dallas, Texas, to have a comprehensive physical at the Cooper Clinic. I had made this appointment months before, and when the time came, I really didn't want the distraction of this trip. I was having a great time with my fast and all the awesome things that were happening to people in our church. I almost postponed my trip, but the Holy Spirit said to me, *Stovall, do not put this off.*

A little reluctantly, I obeyed. Good choice! During my physical the doctors discovered that I had a congenital heart defect called a bicuspid valve and, as a result, my aorta was so enlarged it was life threatening. The cardiologist recommended immediate surgery.

Within two weeks, about when my forty-day fast was to end, I headed to the Mayo Clinic in Minnesota for the operation. I believe it is no coincidence that the entire situation with my heart took place during a season of prayer and fasting. God needed to fill my life with some needed physical healing. The details of the whole process were a chain reaction of small miracles. When I review the course of events during those two weeks, I see the hand of God repeatedly at work.

First, it was a miracle that at a "healthy" forty years of age I even felt led to fly halfway across the country (during a very busy time) to get a thorough physical that included heart scans that weren't part of a regular checkup. I have never had any health problems and have always been in great shape. I even had had my heart checked the previous spring after feeling some discomfort from a pulled muscle in my rib cage while water-skiing. When I went to the hospital, they found nothing. I did a follow-up with the doctor, and he, too, found nothing. He did want to do some more tests, but I was so busy I never got around to it. My heart condition had gone undetected all my life. The very fact that it was discovered was a miracle.

Second, having an enlarged aortic root means I had been at risk of a fatal rupture for many years. The doctor told me there are two things you don't want to do as a young person with this condition because they significantly elevate your risk: play contact sports like football and lift heavy weights.

When I heard that I said, "Are you kidding me? These are the two things I have done almost all of my life!" I played football for ten years and have long been a weight lifter. On top of that, my crazy party life in college had also elevated my risk for rupture.

The doctor said, "Stovall, it's like you have been playing on a busy freeway your entire life, not really paying attention. It's a miracle you have not been hit. You were an accident waiting to happen."

The truth is the hand of God had protected me my whole life, even when

I was running from Him. It is a miracle nothing happened to me. As Proverbs 2:8 says, "[The Lord] preserves the way of His saints."

Third, it is a miracle how quickly they were able to hook me up with a great team of doctors and surgeons who specialize in this type of surgery. Normally, you don't make it to the surgeon I saw at the Mayo Clinic without a long wait.

I am so grateful to God for all He did, and for His favor and protection in that entire situation. As I write this chapter, I am four weeks post op and am amazed at the grace and power of God shown through this trial. All these miracles were an outflow of making room in my life through fasting. I made space and tuned in to God's voice, and He filled my empty space in a way that was above all I could ever ask or think.

> God had protected me my whole life, even when I was running from Him.

HEARING THE VOICE OF GOD

As you can imagine, following the surgery I was in a lot of pain and physical discomfort. There was a process of healing and recovery I had to go through. Needless to say, I had a lot of time to think and contemplate different areas of my life. While I would never want to go through anything like that again, I wouldn't trade the time I spent with God in that solitude for anything. There were no cell phones, no pressures, no crowds. Some nights, especially in the ICU, it was only God and me.

What I realized during that time was that even though I am disciplined at spending time with God, I had still let too many voices and distractions creep in on my time with Him. I had not been getting in that place of solitude where I could really download God's voice and hear only Him. When it was just the two of us in that hospital room, man, how clear the voice of God was! It was then that I heard God tell me as clear as day: *Stovall, teach My people how to seek Me. They have to hear My voice.*

I feel like the first ten years of my ministry in Celebration Church was life with Jesus in the fast lane. I ran so hard and so fast. My relationship with God was great, but the church grew so rapidly I had to sprint to keep up. I suppose it's okay to be in the fast lane, as long as you are making regular rest stops to get alone with God. But it's so easy to let the other voices, business, and pressures of ministry crowd out the voice of God.

Even Jesus had to create space for His Father to fill. He often went away to a deserted place where He could pray and hear the voice of His Father (Luke 4:42). We need to do the same thing, because there are many powerful and intimate experiences with God that we will only enjoy in a "deserted place."

> Even though I am disciplined at spending time with God, I had still let too many voices and distractions creep in on my time with Him.

Both Moses and John the Baptist were in the desert when they heard God's voice. I'm not saying you have to get a machete and hack your way out in the wilderness or travel to some desert somewhere, but whether it's in your car, in your bedroom, or wherever, *get alone with God* so you can hear the voice of your heavenly Father.

Hearing from God doesn't need to take a long time, but neither can it be rushed. You don't have to pray and cry out to God for two hours a day every single day of the week to hear His voice. Reading your Bible doesn't mean it has to be four chapters a day. I think a lot of times we make this more complicated than it really is. What you do need is a time that is set aside, a time for nothing but you and God, and you need to guard that time. Pick a place that works for you where you can really get alone with God and detach from the usual distractions. Come prepared to hear from Him, having things like your Bible, a pen, a highlighter, and a journal readily available. Have a worship CD or your iPod within reach too.

In the "Awakening 21-Day Plan," I'll go into more detail on this and share with you some of the things I do to keep my time with God fresh and new, but also simple and sustainable. I'll show you how to make Bible reading, personal devotion and prayer, and fasting a part of your regular lifestyle. It really doesn't have to be complicated. You have to find out what works for you and create space for God.

As you create space either through giving, praying, or fasting, there's no doubt in my mind that God will respond and fill that space in a powerful way. But the key is to remain intentional about keeping those spaces open throughout the year. How different would your life look if you took one day a week to fast and create space for God? What if you made a commitment to prioritize giving consistently? What if you read God's Word and prayed on a regular basis? We create space for God through seeking Him. That is what Awakening is all about, creating space for God.

I challenge you to be intentional about creating space. Remember, God is a filler, not a forcer. He's not going to push His way into your life—your family, career, or finances. But when you create the space, He will fill it in a fresh and powerful way.

In summary, here are the four foundational steps to an awakening:
- experiencing surrender
- experiencing passion for God
- experiencing God's goodness
- creating space for God to fill

Our problem is that we seriously underestimate how God wants to help us in life. He's the God of the impossible. Let's give Him some room to do His thing!

An Awakening Story

Create Space for God and He Will Provide

Over a period of drawing closer to God, I felt Him prompting me to be obedient in the area of tithing. My husband and I had been giving to the church, but it was somewhat inconsistent. We were recently married and had just moved to a new city where my husband could accept a new job offer. He had gone to school to be an accountant, but this new prospect was in sales, a field much different and less financially predictable than his previous career path.

I let my husband know that I really felt God wanted us to tithe 10 percent of our gross income. Yet his having just started this new job and still being a financially disciplined accountant at heart, 10 percent of our total gross seemed like a big leap from where we were. We started giving a little more, and I kept praying that we would start tithing the full 10 percent. I didn't let go of what God was prompting me in my heart to do, but I also didn't want to be the one to force it on my husband. I knew it would have to be God placing this on his heart.

We joined the awakening fast, and one of the things I committed to God in prayer was to align both my husband and me with His perfect will in every area of our lives. A few weeks later, my husband told me God moved in his heart not only to tithe on our total gross income, but to give over and above our tithe to the building campaign. I was blown away!

As soon as we took that leap of faith, everything changed for us. We had moved to this new city with very little reserves, yet almost immediately after we started tithing, things took a turn. God began blessing my husband at his new job so much that in a very short period of time, he went from being one of the newest, most inexperienced people on his team to consistently being the company's highest-ranking sales rep in the entire country.

By being obedient to what God had asked us to do, He has blessed us so much more than we could have ever imagined!

—T. LOGERO

PART TWO

THE AWAKENING
LIFESTYLE

6

Unlocking the Secrets
of Prayer

HAVE YOU EVER BEEN AROUND SOMEONE who's fervent in prayer? I mean a real prayer person? I'm talking about someone who can really shake the gates of heaven. People who pray fervently love praying so much that it can almost be intimidating to be near them.

I had a couple of those people in my life when I was growing up. One woman in particular was the mom of a football buddy of mine from high school. She was always praying and it was intense. Many times my buddy and I would walk through the front door of his house and all of a sudden this hand would—*whack!*—slap me across the forehead. Before I knew it, his mom was already praying over me. And I mean major prayer! If you went out to eat with her, you'd better hold on. When she blessed the food, it was not a simple "God is great, God is good" kind of prayer. No way! I'm talking intense, fervent, loud, long, and sometimes embarrassing prayer.

I wasn't walking with God then, and even though I thought this lady was "out there," watching and listening to her pray left an impression on me. She had access to something that I could tell was real. I knew she was touching God.

My aunt Tricia is also a praying woman. When I was young she always prayed for me and told me about God. To this day, I still remember some of the specific prayers she spoke over me about God's purpose for my life. I believe the prayers of these two women were instrumental in my coming to Christ.

As believers, we know prayer is important…and powerful. With Jesus as our example, we know from the New Testament that prayer was a significant aspect of His life and ministry. The Bible records multiple times that He withdrew alone to pray to His Father. The connection between His power and prayer life was clearly evident to the disciples, prompting them to ask Him, "Lord, teach us to pray" (Luke 11:1). They knew that if they could unlock the secret of prayer, all the teaching, preaching, healing, and miracles would follow. I believe the power Jesus demonstrated in His public ministry was directly related to the prayer life He had in private.

> I believe the power Jesus demonstrated in His public ministry was directly related to the prayer life He had in private.

I'm sure many of us would like to have a stronger, more effective prayer life. Who wouldn't? However, I think for most of us prayer can seem mysterious. We know the significance of it, we want to get better at it, but if we are honest, we don't totally understand how it works.

For example, have you ever prayed and prayed about something, yet nothing happened? Then on another occasion maybe you barely offered up a little prayer about something in the car on the way to work, and all of a sudden—*bam!*—God answered immediately. It's understandable why these experiences raise questions, such as:

- *Why does God answer some prayers so quickly?*
- *Do I need to pray a certain way or include certain words?*
- *Why don't some of my really important prayers get answered?*
- *How many times do I have to pray before seeing an answer?*
- *If I just obey the Word and walk in faith, how much do my prayers really matter?*

As always the first place to go for answers to these questions is the Word of God. Initially, it might seem there are contradictory stories and parables in the Bible about prayer. For example, Jesus said, essentially, "Don't think that you're going to be heard because of your many words" (Matthew 6:7), and, "Your Father knows exactly what you need even before you ask him!" (Matthew 6:8, NLT). Then there's the story of the persistent widow (Luke 18:1–8), and other situations in the Bible where people prayed several times. No wonder we ask, "What's the deal?" and "How does prayer work?"

THE THREEFOLD CORD OF PREVAILING PRAYER

I want to unpack some of the secrets I've discovered to powerful, prevailing prayer. Let's start off by looking at this well-known verse about prayer from James 5:16: "The effective, fervent prayer of a righteous man avails much."

When I first read that, I asked myself, *What in the world does* avail *mean?* It is actually the Greek word *ischyo,* which means "to exert or wield power; to be a force; to have strength to overcome." Wow! That definitely sounds like the kind of prayers I want—ones that are a force to be reckoned with. However, notice that James does not say *all* prayers avail much. There's a qualification for which ones do, and that is what we must understand.

Ecclesiastes 4:12 says, "Though one may be overpowered by another, two can withstand him. And a threefold cord is not quickly broken." There is a threefold cord of prevailing prayer that is not quickly or easily broken. The cords are *effectiveness, fervency,* and *righteousness.* As a New Testament believer, you already have the righteous cord "through faith in Christ" (Philippians 3:9). Therefore, if you can get ahold of the other principles of effective and fervent prayer, it will change your life.

In a previous chapter we talked about having the right mind-set and focusing on the goodness, greatness, and glory of God. God is your Father and He loves you. He wants to talk to you, and He wants you to talk to Him about everything, big and small. Psalm 37:23 says, "The LORD directs the steps of the godly. He delights in every detail of their lives" (NLT). Just like you would want to talk to a friend or a loved one about what's going on in your life, be it good or challenging, there's nothing God doesn't want you to talk to Him about. Remember, though, to approach prayer with a clear understanding of the goodness, greatness, and glory of God locked firmly in place.

> God wants you to talk to Him about everything, big and small.

Like other things we have talked about, prayer can easily become about our performance rather than about knowing God. When that happens, prayer turns into a legalistic obligation, and the joy goes right out of it. An example of a legalistic attitude toward prayer would be thinking you have to pray each day without fail at the same time, for a certain amount of time, and according to a certain format. And if you don't, look out—God will be unhappy with you.

Such a performance mentality actually sets you up for an inconsistent prayer life, because every time you fail to meet your standards, you will fall under condemnation, and instead of looking forward to your next prayer time, it will seem a joyless burden. Instead of coming to the throne of God boldly and confidently, you will come apologizing for missing your prayer time for a day or two or for cutting it short by a few minutes.

Just as we need to keep our relationship with God fresh, we must also keep our prayer time fresh. It is time to have an awakening in our prayer life! Right now, if you are feeling negative toward prayer, I want you to stop reading for a moment and ask yourself why you feel this way. It's likely that deep down you have a legalistic mind-set about prayer. So as we look at the aspects of a confident and powerful prayer life, I want you to remember that the primary goal of prayer is relationship building—to draw near to God.

RIGHTEOUS PRAYER

As we discussed previously, under the New Covenant of grace, the blood of Jesus has made you righteous. In other words, once you accept Jesus as your

Savior, you are in "right standing" with God (Romans 8:33, NLT). You are completely forgiven and justified in God's sight (Romans 3:24). It is just as if you have never sinned. Jesus qualified us to come into God's presence; however, we do not come based on our own merit. We come through the name of Jesus. Because of Him we have incredible authority when we pray.

Jesus told His disciples when they pray to the Father, to do so in His name (John 15:16; 16:23–24). Do you understand what that means? Jesus has given us His name to use! Just imagine if some billionaire gave you his credit cards and authorized you to use his bank accounts. You could use his name and his resources to get whatever you needed. Wow, that would be a blast! But here is the catch: everything you did with his money needed to be in line with his tastes and his values.

> When you pray in the name of Jesus, it has the same power as if Jesus were praying Himself.

God hears you every time you pray in the name of Jesus. When Jesus gave us His name, He was giving us total access to His incredible power and unlimited resources. *When you pray in the name of Jesus, it has the same power as if Jesus were praying Himself.* The difference between us and Jesus is that Jesus is always in complete alignment with His Father. This is why periodic seasons of fasting are so important. Fasting is the quickest way to really get in alignment with God.

Thus, the first cord to praying prayers that avail much is *praying in alignment with God's will.* When you pray in the name of Jesus according to the will of the Father, God will intervene in your situation. When you are in alignment with God's purpose, you can ask whatever you want and God will do it (John 16:23–24). I will discuss how we get into alignment in a coming section.

EFFECTIVE PRAYER

On occasion people have told me, "Okay, Stovall, I believe God hears my prayers, but it seems like a lot of times His answer to me is no."

Trust me—if that's the case, be grateful for it. Even though we may not see it at the time, God knows what is best for you and me. If you are a parent, you know that saying no to a child who wants to play on a busy street is a very loving response.

Many times in my walk with God I have asked God to do something and He didn't. Looking back, I'm so thankful! However, I honestly believe that most of the time, we can actually know beforehand if God's answer is going to be yes or no. This brings us to the second cord of prevailing prayer: *effective prayer.*

Can you know if God will say yes to your prayer?

Wouldn't that give you the confidence, faith, and persistence to keep praying? But how can we really know that? And if God's going to say yes, how many times do we need to pray to see the prayer answered?

Effective prayer starts with knowing what the Word of God says about your situation. We have to continually renew our minds through the Word of God. Jesus said, "If…My words abide in you, you will ask what you desire, and it shall be done for you" (John 15:7). He didn't say when it would be done, but He did say that it would be done.

Hebrews 4:12 says this about the Word of God: "For the word of God is living and powerful, and sharper than any two-edged sword, piercing even to the division of soul and spirit, and of joints and marrow, and is a discerner of the thoughts and intents of the heart."

The Word of God is *living.* That means regardless of what you're facing in life, God can speak to you through His Word and by the power of the Holy Spirit in every situation. Prayer is an instrument of life, and thereby has the power to produce life in your situation.

The Word of God is *powerful.* It is a weapon you want to fight with, not against. If we want our prayers to be effective, we need to align them with the Word of God. When we do, we align them with the life-giving power of the Word as well. This is when your prayers become bold, because they carry power and authority.

The Word of God is *truth.* When we read it with an open heart, it discerns our truest thoughts and motives. It is like a mirror that reflects light and truth, allowing us to examine our intentions (James 1:23).

Righteous prayer is based not on our own righteousness but on the righteousness of Jesus. *Effective prayer* is based not on our own authority but on the authority of the Word of God. A righteous person praying an effective prayer is a believer in Jesus praying a Word-based prayer. Can you now see how prayer is actually less about us and more about glorifying God? It is not as much about getting from God as it is about aligning our self with what God already wants to do. Many times, though, we can get so focused on our own comfort or our own preferences that we don't even take the time to examine ourselves or see what God's Word has to say about our situation.

Many young, single people attend Celebration Church. I am oftentimes asked to pray for a relationship with a boyfriend or girlfriend because, "We just can't seem to get along," or, "We fight all the time," or, "We can't agree on anything!" As we continue talking, I find out that the person wanting prayer is dating a nonbeliever. *Are you kidding me?* I think. Even though this happens often enough, it always catches me by surprise. God has already made it plain in His Word that a follower of Christ shouldn't be in this type of relationship with an unbeliever. This is called being "unequally yoked" (2 Corinthians 6:14).

Can you see how silly it is to ask God to bless something He has already clearly directed us to not do? Going against His revealed will can only produce pain and dis-

> We have a part to play in the effectiveness of our prayers, and it has to do with alignment.

comfort in our lives. How in the world could such a prayer have any power? In fact, not only are these prayers out of alignment with the Word of God, but the power and authority of the Word are directly opposed to them. Talk about double trouble from the get-go!

As another example, take the principle of putting God first. God's Word is very clear that we should do this. In Matthew 6:33 Jesus said, "Seek first the kingdom of God and His righteousness, and all these things shall be added to you." The entire context of this passage concerns the arena of provision. Many times people will plead with God for a financial breakthrough, yet they neglect to put Him first in a practical way by tithing.

We have a part to play in the effectiveness of our prayers, and it has to do with alignment. We have to align our prayers with the Word, and we may also need to align some aspects of our lives with His Word. When we don't pray according to the will of God as revealed in His Word, our prayers will lack direction, confidence, and power. That's a formula for certain ineffectiveness.

FERVENT PRAYER

The third and final cord of prevailing prayer is *fervency*. Remember our verse from James 5:16: "The effective, fervent prayer of a righteous man avails much." I believe this is the aspect of prevailing prayer that Christians struggle most with. A lot of believers I know have the righteous part down— I mean, what other option do we really have but to pray in Jesus' name, right? They are also sincere and really want the revealed will of God to be the norm in their lives, even though they may struggle sometimes. But fervency is different—it's about passion to glorify God.

Our motivation in prayer should not just be centered on ourselves so we can have what we need. God thrives where He can prove Himself. He wants to be glorified in and through us. And He wants to be glorified in the earth. But God will share that glory and honor with no one. He deserves nothing less than all the glory, all the honor, and all the praise.

Think about the prayers in your life. Do you just want to be happy in your marriage or do you want God to be glorified in your marriage? Do you merely want your kids to be nice and not get in trouble or do you want God to be glorified in their lives? Do you simply want to get out of your financial mess and feel some relief or do you want God to be glorified in your finances? Do you want Him to be glorified in your business and career? When the whole focus of our prayers is only our relief and happiness, not the glory of God, we will become easily discouraged when we don't see a quick answer to our prayers.

Yes, there are things we all need and want. Most of the time those are good things, and our heavenly Father wants to bless us with those things. He wants us to be happy (Psalm 84:11). But God has created us in such a way that we cannot experience true fulfillment and happiness unless we are living for His glory. Read that verse again: "Seek first the kingdom of God and His righteousness, and all these things shall be added to you" (Matthew 6:33).

> So many of our prayers are really all about us and experiencing relief.

Do you see the difference? The motive of our prayers should be for the glory of God regardless of our personal comfort or preference. So many of our prayers are really all about us and experiencing relief. And while many times God in His mercy answers those prayers how we hope He will, if you want to pray with confidence and know that God is going to answer yes, glorifying God has to be your first motive.

That's the key: do we have a passion for the glory of God? I believe this is the number one thing believers today are missing from their prayer lives and why so many prayers are not answered the way they hope.

We really can't have fervency in our prayers without having a spiritual hunger and fire for God. This is why awakening is so important in igniting your prayer life. Fervent prayer requires passion for God. Fervent prayer comes from a position of affection toward God. As long as we stay in a lethargic, sleepy state, we will not have passion for the glory of God. The cares of the world and the desires of the flesh will numb us and our prayer lives will be hindered. In my experience, *lack of fervency in prayer is the first sign that my soul is in need of a fresh awakening.* As I start to drift and prayer feels more like an obligation than a passionately driven affection to glorify God, I know it's time to initiate the process of renewal through prayer and fasting. I need awakening.

AND STILL NO ANSWER?

Another question many people ask me about prayer is, "How many times should I pray about something? I've prayed and prayed and prayed and nothing is happening. I am a child of God, praying in the name of Jesus and according to His Word. I want God to be glorified in this situation, so if God is hearing my prayers, why is there no answer?"

Sometimes we do everything right, yet we still find ourselves with seemingly no answer from God. Because you have to wait does not mean He didn't hear you or that He's saying no. Most times it is just the opposite. Waiting on God is necessary because most answers to prayer involve a much bigger picture than we know or understand.

The answers to our prayers can involve a process of God setting the stage and moving in a supernatural way. Every answer to prayer is typically a preparation for what will happen next. God is not just looking at point A to point B; He is looking at A to Z. He is the Alpha and the Omega (Revelation 1:8). He sees the end from the beginning (Isaiah 46:10). Much of waiting on God has to do with God preparing us for the challenges or blessings that the answer to our prayer will bring.

Waiting on God to answer our prayers is not a passive thing like waiting at the doctor's office or the DMV. Waiting on God includes engaging Him in a process that will make room for His kingdom to come and His will to be done on earth, as it already is in heaven. Many times we look at the answer to our prayer as the end, when in fact, the answer to the prayer is just a means: God is preparing us, stretching us, expanding us, and strengthening us for what the answer to that prayer will bring.

If you're in a season of waiting on God, I encourage you not to lose hope. Engage the process and remain confident that God has heard you, loves you, and wants only the best for your life: "And we know that all things work together for good to those who love God, to those who are the called according to His purpose" (Romans 8:28).

Maybe you have always thought that having a lifestyle of prevailing prayer was for other people—people like my aunt or my friend's mom. Maybe you have told yourself that you're just not a prayer person. But each of us, every Christian, is a candidate for a life of prevailing prayer. As a child of God and a follower of Christ, you *are praying* as a righteous person. As you pray according to the

> As a child of God and a follower of Christ, you *are praying* as a righteous person.

Word of God, your prayers *do carry* authority and power. They are effective. And if your passion is to glorify God, then your prayers are *fervent*. These are the types of prayers that will avail much.

Righteous prayer is based not on our own righteousness but on the righteousness of Jesus. *Effective prayer* is based not on our own authority but on the authority of the Word of God. *Fervent prayer* is based not on our own comforts or preferences but on the purpose of glorifying God.

When we pray according to these three, we can have the confidence that God will say yes to our prayers. Keep praying until you see the answer. You will see it! Don't give up, but be persistent in prayer (1 Thessalonians 5:17) and remember that through faith and endurance we inherit the promises of God (Hebrews 6:12).

Next, we're going to discover the most powerful companion to prayer. It is the atomic bomb of our spiritual weapons, yet it is one of the most unfamiliar and least practiced disciplines of believers. Get ready as we discover the incredible power of renewing our souls through new school fasting.

An Awakening Story

The Mountain Moved

My wife and I had dreamed of one day owning and running our own business. In the spring of 2005 an opportunity to purchase a business was presented to us. We researched it and had a local small business development center evaluate the opportunity. Then, in June 2005 we purchased it with a combination of cash and a promissory note from the previous owners. That meant that we had invested our life's savings and were personally responsible for a $175,000 promissory note. We also took over the facility lease agreement, operating expenses, and payroll.

We quickly realized that the business was not turning a profit. Every month our expenses were outpacing revenue. That meant that we were unable to draw a salary from the business. It was an incredible time of testing and learning. We were tested on all fronts—from our finances to our marriage. Once we realized that we were not going to be able to continue running the business, we tried to reach an agreement with the previous owners to turn it back over to them, but they declined. The next call I received was from their attorney. To make a long story short, we had to hire a business attorney to explore our options. At the same time we met with a bankruptcy attorney, fearing that might be our only option.

In July 2006 our attorney advised us that he had negotiated a deal for us to hand the keys back over to the previous owners as we were now in default of our promissory note to them. We thought this meant that the promissory note was being cancelled, but it did not. We were still going to be responsible for repaying the note. It was a very dark time, challenging us mentally and physically, as well as testing our faith in God. In January 2007, we participated in the Awakening: 21 Days of Prayer and Fasting and committed the business situation to God while spending a lot of time in prayer and learning to truly surrender. We believed that even though our faith only seemed to be the size of a mustard seed, that God could move the mountain in front of us.

We broke the fast on a Friday night and there was still no sign of movement in our situation. We felt a little down and disappointed, but believed God had heard our prayers.

Little did we know that that very Friday the previous owners had filed a form with the IRS, which in essence released us of the $175,000 debt owed. It was as if the weight of the world had been lifted off our shoulders. God had once again proven Himself faithful.

Walking through this process of praying, fasting, and seeking God was a journey that left us stronger, wiser, and with complete trust and faith in Him and Him alone. Our relationship with God and each other had grown even deeper during this time of testing. We know that God can and will make a way where there seems to be no way. We learned that we cannot look at our circumstances through natural eyes. When we spend time in prayer and fasting, we begin to see things differently and it allows God to move supernaturally.

JONATHAN MACARTHUR

7

New School Fasting

IT'S TIME TO GET A NEW OUTLOOK ON FASTING. When practiced the right way, fasting is something everyone should enjoy. That's right...*enjoy*!

I know what you might be thinking...*Isn't fasting for emergencies or for the really holy people?* No, fasting is for every follower of Jesus! Let me explain.

Too many people I know fast with a strict mind-set that focuses on abstaining. The fasting I'm talking about here is different. Of course it involves abstaining from some foods, but the mind-set is completely different. I will eventually show you how to find your fasting zone where you experience minimum physical emptiness with maximum spiritual fullness.

I know several people who, once they began to fast correctly with a New Testament mind-set, did not want to end their fast even after their twenty-one days. Fasting is one of the most powerful spiritual weapons believers can use, yet many Christians have never experienced it. There is a common misperception that fasting is for serious Christians or only for times of crisis. Some even think fasting is an Old Testament thing. This couldn't be further from the truth.

I can say this with total confidence: *There is a closeness to God that you simply will not experience from prayer or personal devotions alone. You must fast.* You get a greater revelation of God's Word when you fast that you simply cannot get any other way. Disconnecting from the distractions of the world through fasting, and connecting into the power and presence of God through prayer brings a supernatural freshness and newness to our souls.

Jesus clearly said, "When you fast" (Matthew 6:16), and "This kind can come out by nothing but prayer and fasting" (Mark 9:29). That basically means some things only change when you fast. Jesus Himself fasted (Matthew 4:1–2). To be blunt, questioning or overlooking the necessity of fasting would be equivalent to questioning prayer, or reading God's Word, or helping those in need. We simply can't afford to dismiss a spiritual practice that the Bible endorses. We must learn how to wield this mighty spiritual weapon. It is one of the greatest gifts God has given us for renewing our soul.

Like many other things we've discussed, the primary purpose of fasting is to help us draw closer to God. But how we view fasting, and essentially how we fast, makes all the difference in how we will benefit from it. I've come across people who have tried fasting but had an Old Testament or what I call an old school mind-set about it. Because of that their fasting experience was drudgery and lacked the freshness, strength, and enjoyment fasting is intended to bring.

> There is a closeness to God that you simply will not experience from prayer or personal devotions alone. You must fast.

As you will see, there are important differences between fasting in the Old Covenant and fasting in the New Covenant that we must first discover. The purpose for which we fast has changed, and so has the manner in which we do it. There was an old school way to fast, but now there's a new school way, and Jesus explained the difference.

FASTING IN THE NEW COVENANT

Fasting was the topic of conversation one day when Jesus was talking to some of John the Baptist's disciples. These impassioned friends of John wanted to know why Jesus and His disciples were not following the Jewish custom of fasting. Jesus responded, telling them how fasting was about to change and what purpose fasting would have in the life of the New Testament believer:

> Then the disciples of John came to Him, saying, "Why do we and the Pharisees fast often, but Your disciples do not fast?"
>
> And Jesus said to them, "Can the friends of the bridegroom mourn as long as the bridegroom is with them? But the days will come when the bridegroom will be taken away from them, and then they will fast. No one puts a piece of unshrunk cloth on an old garment; for the patch pulls away from the garment, and the tear is made worse. Nor do they put new wine into old wineskins, or else the wineskins break, the wine is spilled, and the wineskins are ruined. But they put new wine into new wineskins, and both are preserved."
> (Matthew 9:14–17)

Surprisingly, many people take this to mean that Jesus didn't think fasting was necessary. That's a complete misunderstanding. Jesus didn't say that we shouldn't fast. In fact, from the language He used ("then they will fast"), it seems He fully expected His disciples to return to the practice of fasting after His ascent to heaven. What Jesus said was that the old way and the new way could not mix. The New Covenant of grace was about to be established, and everything was going to change, fasting included. The old reasons for which they fasted before would not mix with the new meaning and purpose, and He explained why.

Jesus gave two illustrations to help us clearly understand this concept of old versus new. First, He compared it to putting new cloth on an old garment. Secondly, He compared old wineskins and new wineskins. This was a very intentional illustration, because in the Bible, oil and wine are symbolic of the Holy Spirit.

Back in Jesus' day, wine was stored not in bottles but in containers called wineskins. To hold freshly made wine, the wineskins needed to be soft and pliable, because when the fresh wine began to ferment, it would cause the wineskin to expand. So the wineskin had to be able to expand with the wine. Old wineskins wouldn't work, because they had become hard, brittle, and inflexible. An old wineskin filled with new wine would crack and break once the wine began to expand, and the fresh, new wine would spill out.

Now think of this as it applies to a New Testament believer. When we are saved, we receive the Holy Spirit (the wine). He comes and dwells on the inside of us (the wineskin). Remember earlier we discussed how God is a filler, and when He fills the spaces in our lives, He multiplies or brings expansion to them. I want you to get this picture. There are fresh, new things that God wants to do in your life, new works of the Holy Spirit, expanding works that He's predestined for your life, but you need a new "wineskin" to contain them.

You need a new wineskin to move forward in God's purpose for your life. But what most people don't realize is you don't get a new wineskin just once—when you get saved. *We must repeatedly receive new wineskins so that God's work can continue to expand in our lives.* The old wineskin represents old seasons, staleness, stiffness, even hardheartedness. The old and stale will not be able to contain the new and fresh.

> You need a new wineskin to move forward in God's purpose for your life.

Fasting gives us a new wineskin. As we draw closer to God through periodic seasons of prayer and fasting, He renews us, preparing us to contain the fresh, new things He wants to bring to our lives. But it's very important that we have the right mind-set about fasting, because we cannot mix the old with the new. We simply cannot have an Old Covenant mind-set about fasting. If you are going to fast, it has to be done through the filter and principles of the New Covenant.

OLD SCHOOL VERSUS NEW SCHOOL

You'll find many accounts of people—even whole nations—fasting in the Old Testament for different reasons. Primarily, fasting had to do with mourning or getting God to intervene during a crisis. It had to do with convincing God to change His mind and obtaining favor from Him. For example, in Joel 2:12–14 the people said, essentially, "We're going to seek God with fasting and with mourning and maybe God will have mercy on us."

We know the story of Jonah and the impending doom that was coming to Nineveh. Back then people also fasted to show sorrow and repentance for their sins. So the people of Nineveh said, "Let's fast and maybe God will change His mind" (Jonah 3:5–9).

I want to make it very clear that under the New Covenant, fasting is not to get God to change His mind about something. Fasting is also not something we do to obtain favor or forgiveness. After you receive Jesus Christ as your Lord and Savior, your past, present, and future sins have already been forgiven! You don't need to fast to obtain favor or receive mercy, because through Jesus you live in a continual state of God's mercy. Instead, fasting is a way of celebrating the goodness of God and that because of Jesus we have already received God's mercy, forgiveness, and favor.

Under the Old Covenant, the entire mind-set was to "do in order to become." But under the New Covenant, the operative principle is "you already are, therefore act like it"—rejoice and celebrate that Christ has set you free (Galatians 5:1)! You don't have to fast for mercy; instead, celebrate the mercy given to you as a free gift through your relationship with Christ. Under the New Covenant you don't fast to obtain the Lord's favor, because you perpetually live in the favor of the Lord. Do you see the difference?

Jesus asked John's disciples, "Can the friends of the bridegroom mourn as long as the bridegroom is with them? But the days will come when the bridegroom will be taken away from them, and then they will fast." Notice He did not say that when the

> Under the Old Covenant, the entire mind-set was to "do in order to become." Under the New Covenant, the operative principle is "you already are, therefore act like it."

bridegroom is taken away His disciples would mourn and fast. He said they would fast. He said this in the context of new wine. Unlike old school fasting, new school fasting would not be connected to crisis, mourning, and impending judgment.

New school fasting is not about mourning or sadness, but it is about celebrating the goodness of God. As believers, our longing for Jesus is accompanied by the joy He sent us through the Holy Spirit. It is not a sad mourning but an expectant, joyful longing.

While certain principles of fasting are the same, such as drawing near to God, the purpose and experience are completely different. Old Testament believers did not have the Holy Spirit or the living Word dwelling inside of them as New Covenant believers do (Romans 8:9, 11). Their bodies were not temples of the Holy Spirit either (1 Corinthians 3:16).

> Fasting is not about mourning or sadness; it's about celebrating the goodness of God.

Jesus said that when He was taken away, His disciples would fast. But new school fasting is all about *celebrating* Christ and allowing the Holy Spirit on the inside of us to expand to a greater degree as we shut down the natural man and engage the spiritual man. We have no need to mourn for Jesus, because through the Holy Spirit, He is always with us—He will never leave us or forsake us (Hebrews 13:5). Fasting will not do much for you if you have an old school mentality. You must grab on to the new school principles of fasting. It will change your life. God will bring a freshness and newness to your soul that will prepare you to receive the incredible, new, expanding thing He already has planned for you.

FASTING GETS THE GUNK OUT

As we live our lives, over time we get all "gunked up." While our spirit is eternally made new through Christ (2 Corinthians 4:16), our soul, which is the intersection of our mind, will, and emotions, can become weighed down, heavy, negative, and sluggish.

The constant demands on our mind, the distractions, and the noise can weigh us down and put us in a spiritual fog. Life has a way of stacking on the pressure and pain, which causes our emotions to get out of whack. As we get tired and weighed down, our conscience can become desensitized, not really bothered by the things that once convicted us. God's voice is slowly muffled, and we begin to lose our passion for Him. The fire within dims, and we shift into autopilot, operating from a position of obligation or routine in our relationship with God, instead of one of affection and fervor.

Even if we are going to church, reading our Bible, and worshiping, there are times when we need to give our souls a good spring cleaning to make them fresh again. We've got to get the gunk out of God's temple so we can hear His voice clearly and prepare ourselves for the new things He wants to do in and through us. This is what fasting does. It is the secret key to "Never be lacking in zeal, but keep your spiritual fervor, serving the Lord" (Romans 12:11, NIV). Fasting gives us a new wineskin and gets the fire back in our relationship with Him.

Fasting hits the reset button of your soul. For example, think about your home. Most people typically clean their house once a week (okay, if you're a single guy, maybe it's more like once a month). As you maintain your home, from week to week things look pretty good on the surface. But even so, every now and then you probably set aside some time to do some deeper cleaning.

> Fasting hits the reset button of your soul.

As you look on top of the ceiling fan blades, for example, you notice the grime and dust and think, *Oh, gross!* You realize that all this time, while the fan's been spinning around, it's been slinging all this gunk and dust around the room, on your furniture, and on your kids. Ugh! Disgusting!

Then, as you think you're making some traction, you get to the windowsills. You pull back the curtains and, *oh no,* what is that? Dead bugs? Fly guts?

What's been going on back here? It's like a lizard's been massacring flies. And what's all this black muck underneath the windowsill? It's time to pull out all the heavy-duty cleaning gear and set off an atomic cleaning bomb in that place!

As you start to dig deep, you realize your home that seemed so clean on the surface was actually pretty filthy. But after a good, deep cleaning, your home is fresh again, clean and restored. That's the same thing fasting does for our souls. It's like a deep cleaning that gets rid of all the gunk that has built up unnoticed over time.

I experienced this in another way while on a hunting trip. I'm an avid duck hunter, and each year I like to take a trip (or two) back to my home state of Louisiana. I have always taken pretty good care of my shotgun. I give it a basic cleaning every now and then and always wipe it down after a hunt. Throughout the season, the gun seems to shoot fine. It works and appears reasonably clean. But a few years ago at the end of the hunting season, I decided to take the gun apart and really give it a deep, thorough cleaning. I'll never forget what happened.

> Fasting is like a deep cleaning that gets rid of all the gunk that has built up unnoticed over time.

In order to clean the trigger mechanism, I detached it and dropped it into a bowl of gasoline. After a few seconds I was shocked. I didn't think it was that dirty, but immediately all of this gunk and dirt came to the top like a cloud of black smoke. After seeing how dirty it actually was, I couldn't believe the gun had fired at all. How did all that gunk get in there?

That's similar to how our mind and emotions can get soiled. Our souls can actually get gunked up through the cares, concerns, human nature, and pressures of life. The world we live in is a gunk-ifier. We may go through each day thinking everything is fine, but when we fast, it's like dipping that trigger mechanism into that gasoline. We dip our souls into the fire of God and come out fresh and clean! We experience newness again. Life has a fresh smell and taste to it, and our passion is renewed for the Lord. We are awakened to God's Spirit on the inside of us. We truly experience the new wine or "newness of life" (Romans 6:4).

Can you see how we need that deep cleaning in our mind, emotions, and soul? To receive the new things God wants to bring into our lives, we have to periodically hit the reset button. This is what I call experiencing a newness of soul. That's when God can really begin to take you "from glory to glory" (2 Corinthians 3:18). We advance in our relationship with God in an accelerated way and begin to supernaturally maximize our effectiveness in moving His kingdom forward. Man, what a powerful gift we have been given through fasting!

Ready—Reset—Go!

Fasting is a huge key to awakening and revolutionizing your walk with God. I will give you several practical how-tos and types of fasts in a later chapter, but for now know that God is passionate for you and He wants you to be passionate for Him. The more passionate you are for God, the more true joy you experience. Worldly gunk is the enemy to spiritual passion. If you want to experience everything God has in store for you and keep your fire for God, you need to regularly do some spring cleaning in your soul.

I hope you're ready to hit the reset button and experience the freshness of God in your soul. Next, I'm going to show you how fasting releases and prepares you to reach your fullest potential in life. We're going to discuss several other by-products and practical aspects of fasting, all of which will set you on course to live a life of passion.

Remember, passionate Christianity is supposed to be the norm for the believer, not the exception. It's time for an awakening!

> Worldly gunk is the enemy to spiritual passion.

An Awakening Story

A New Direction

A few months after we started attending church, my husband and I heard about the upcoming Awakening 21 Days of Prayer and Fasting. We decided to participate, and our lives have never been the same since.

Up until this point, we knew we were prepared to give ourselves fully to the work of the Lord, but we didn't really know exactly what He had planned for us. It was during that fast that God aligned our hearts with His good and perfect will, and it was so much greater and bigger than we could have ever imagined. Through that season of prayer and fasting God prepared us for what He already had in store. We felt God prompting us to move back to our hometown of Columbus, Ohio, where we launched a Celebration Church extension service that is now reaching the area we grew up in.

Prayer and fasting are now a regular part of our lives. Personally, I now find myself praying and fasting not only for my own spiritual growth but also for the women, future leaders, and my church family in Ohio.

Our passion continues to grow and our mission has become clearly outlined. Now we are using our God-given gifts to grow His kingdom, serve Jesus, and serve others. Through walking out God's plan for our lives, we continue to come alongside those who do not know Him and share God's love.

— KELLI WELSHEIMER

8

Agreement, Alignment, Assignment

ONE OF THE REASONS I THINK prayer and fasting are so powerful when combined is that together they activate a chain reaction where we see God's kingdom manifest on earth.

This sequence is what I call *agreement…alignment…assignment*. When we come into *agreement* with God, we are *aligned* with God's perfect will on earth, as it already is in heaven. When we are aligned with heaven, we find that God can use us in ways we never thought possible. Then we begin to walk in our *assignment*—the purpose God created us to fulfill (Ephesians 2:10).

When we are aligned with God's plan and purpose in heaven, we are propelled forward with unstoppable momentum, because God is always on the move. Fasting is a key to establishing this spiritual momentum, because it brings us into a deeper agreement with God, which brings about a greater alignment with God, which is where all the power of the kingdom is found.

The pattern for agreement, alignment, and assignment is actually found in the first few lines of the Lord's Prayer. And it's no coincidence that this passage of Scripture, where Jesus taught His disciples how to pray, comes right before His teaching on fasting, which I believe further confirms that prayer and fasting go hand in hand:

Our Father in heaven,
Hallowed be Your name.
Your kingdom come.
Your will be done
On earth as it is in heaven. (Matthew 6:9–10)

AGREEMENT

The prophet Amos wrote, "Can two people walk together without agreeing on the direction?" (3:3, NLT). To see God's purposes fulfilled, we must first come into agreement that it is His will we want established, not our own. This ties back in to our very first step in experiencing an awakening: living life completely surrendered to God.

Seeing God's "kingdom come" to the point where His will is done through us here on earth first requires agreement on our part. Notice that the first few words of this prayer are of worship and praise to God. As we discussed earlier, this is focusing on the goodness, greatness, and glory of God: "Our Father in heaven, hallowed be Your name."

Then, after prayer and worship, come the words "Your kingdom come. Your will be done on earth as it is in heaven." We cannot start to see God's kingdom come until we are in agreement with His lordship. Being in agreement with God is a choice on our part. It's a heart attitude that is set on glorifying God. This is where the joy… peace…and fulfillment are. Total surrender is a daily practice, a lifestyle, and one that is sustained through prayer and fasting.

> Total surrender is a daily practice, a lifestyle.

We can come into such a level of agreement and unity with God that we will say as Paul described, "It is no longer I who live, but Christ lives in me" (Galatians 2:20). In other words, Paul said, "I'm in such agreement with God, I'm experiencing so much heaven on earth, that I'm confident I'm in complete alignment with Christ and am carrying out His assignment." Paul was completely surrendered to the lordship of Christ in his life.

But staying in full agreement with God requires periodic times of prayer and fasting. Fasting is not for God; it's for us. We are the ones who need to fast—and not to get what we want or to try and get more from God. We need to fast to go full throttle after what God wants so that we can come into full cooperation (or agreement) with His will.

Remember the Scripture from Matthew 6: "When you [give]…when you pray…and when you fast…" (verses 2, 5, 16). Jesus talked about the blessing and rewards associated with doing those three things because they bring us into agreement with the Father.

Can you be in full agreement with God without giving and praying on a regular basis? No, you really can't. Neither can you walk in full agreement with God without regularly fasting. Do you see my point?

First, we come into agreement with God about the lordship of Christ—that it is for His will and for His glory that we live. Then, His kingdom can be established in our lives. This is the point where we begin walking in alignment with God.

ALIGNMENT

An easy way to describe the kingdom of God is to say it's wherever the rule and reign of Jesus are established. In heaven God's rule and reign are always perfectly established. But to see it demonstrated on earth, we must allow Him to align us with His will as it is in heaven.

Agreement with God brings us to the place where we say, "Yes, Lord. It is for Your glory that I live. I want Your will to be done in my life above all else." Alignment by God is the place where He begins to put things in order so that His kingdom can come into our lives. God begins to bring His power and reveal to us what His perfect will is so we can start moving forward with clear, precise aim. Alignment is the place where we are positioned by coming into agreement with God.

Fasting brings us into greater alignment with God in a way that prayer alone cannot. And it takes regular seasons of prayer and fasting to stay in alignment with God's perfect will. In the book of Acts we see the apostles fasting regularly, and many crucial God-direction moments came when they were fasting.

I can almost hear someone asking, "Stovall, are you saying that in order to come into full alignment with God, I need to fast?"

Yes! That's exactly what I am saying, and Jesus said it too.

One day Jesus went up a mountain (now called the Mount of Transfiguration) to pray, and He took Peter, James, and John with Him (Matthew 17). While there, Jesus was transformed into His glorified state, and Peter, James, and John had a front-row seat. I still can't imagine what that must have been like. These guys had walked with Jesus every day, eaten meals with Him, and listened to Him teach. They were already convinced that He was the Messiah. But then they saw Jesus in a glorified state—what a mind-blowing experience!

> Fasting brings us into greater alignment with God in a way that prayer alone cannot.

As incredible as that was, Jesus did not allow them to just soak in their mountaintop experience. He quickly got their minds focused on kingdom business and got them moving down the mountain. The disciples didn't know it, but a man in desperate need was waiting for them at the bottom of the mountain. This should serve as a reminder to us that our encounters with the glory and presence of God are intended not only to bless us but to fire us up to go out and make a difference by reaching out with compassion to people who are lost and hurting.

The man they encountered was a father in need of a breakthrough for his family. In Matthew 17, we read:

> When they had come to the multitude, a man came to Him, kneeling down to Him and saying, "Lord, have mercy on my son, for he is an

epileptic and suffers severely; for he often falls into the fire and often
into the water. So I brought him to Your disciples, but they could not
cure him." (verses 14–16)

This man's son was epileptic and, by some of the language used here, it
would appear he was suicidal too. The phrase the father used, "falls into"
something, was a euphemism of that day to describe suicide attempts. No
doubt this father was desperate. He loved his son, and I'm sure the pain he
felt was overwhelming.

This man knelt humbly before Jesus, shared with Him the pain of what
his son was going through, and also told Jesus of his efforts to get help. The
man had brought his son to some of Jesus' disciples and they were not able to
cast the demon out. Pay close attention to Jesus' response, and to the dialogue
that takes place with His disciples afterward:

> Then Jesus answered and said, "O faithless and perverse generation,
> how long shall I be with you? How long shall I bear with you? Bring
> him here to Me." And Jesus rebuked the demon, and it came out of
> him; and the child was cured from that very hour.
>
> Then the disciples came to Jesus privately and said, "Why could
> we not cast it out?"
>
> So Jesus said to them, "Because of your unbelief; for assuredly,
> I say to you, if you have faith as a mustard seed, you will say to this
> mountain, 'Move from here to there,' and it will move; and nothing
> will be impossible for you. However, this kind does not go out except
> by prayer and fasting." (verses 17–21)

When the disciples came privately to Jesus and asked, "Why could we
not cast the demon out?" in a word, Jesus told them it was because of their
unbelief. This is the root problem for us as well. We want to experience the
supernatural power of God and see Him move, but we, too, like the disciples
in this story, sometimes operate in unbelief.

The power of God is available to you, as it was available to this boy. The problem was not the demon; the problem was unbelief. So Jesus addressed the unbelief.

The first thing He said was, "O faithless and perverse generation." That might seem a bit harsh, but Jesus wasn't being mean. He used two distinctive words that described the root cause of their unbelief: by "faithless" He meant they were too disconnected from God, and "perverse" meant instead that they were too connected to the world. The disciples were too gunked up! We still have the same problem today. When we are too disconnected from God and too connected to the world and its distractions, the result is always unbelief. Instead of walking in faith, we walk in unbelief, and God's kingdom doesn't manifest with power.

The remedy? Prayer and fasting. Jesus didn't tell His boys just to pray. He said to pray and fast. Both were necessary, because prayer connects us to God and fasting disconnects us from the world.* Together, they bring us into greater alignment with heaven.

When you pray and fast, the first thing that comes out is not the "demon" or the problem; it's the unbelief. Fasting deals with the root cause of unbelief. The demon's coming out, or whatever miracle you need, is just a by-product of your believing in God and walking in faith. When you come into alignment with God, you begin to see His perfect will done in your life, as God has already established it in heaven. God's kingdom and power start to manifest in your earth, and that's when you get to the point

> Prayer connects us to God and fasting disconnects us from the world.

where, as Jesus predicted, you can speak to the mountain that's been causing you so much pain and see it cast into the sea (Mark 11:23)! But to come into this level of alignment with Him so you can see those results, you will need to pray and fast.

---

* Jon Courson, *Jon Courson's Application Commentary: New Testament* (Nashville: Thomas Nelson, 2003), 138.

Fasting really is not about trying to get miracles and breakthroughs from God. It is about aligning yourself with God and what He already wants. We don't fast to get God to change something. We fast so that we are changed and come into a greater level of faith.

God has already given us everything we need for living a godly life (2 Peter 1:3). We actually don't need to get anything from God; we just need to learn how to walk in what He gave us when we got saved.

There's another very important thing I want to point out. When the disciples were faced with this crisis, because of their unbelief, or misalignment, they were unprepared to deal with the challenge at hand. Notice when Jesus was faced with the crisis, He didn't have to stop and go on a quick three-day fast to solve the problem. He was already in such alignment with His Father in heaven that He knew what the Father's will was. Fasting aligns you with God and prepares you before the crisis even hits. Jesus was basically telling the disciples, "You need to pray and fast before you encounter the crisis." He was saying that prayer and fasting are part of our preparation as believers to destroy the words of the Evil One. Prayer and fasting should be proactive, not reactive.

Through fasting we shut down our natural man so the spiritual man can rise up. That's awakening! We get what God has deposited in us working on the outside. We align the outside with what's on the inside. We starve unbelief and feed faith. We move our earth into alignment with God's heaven where now anything can happen and "all things are possible to him who believes" (Mark 9:23).

I have great news for you: you don't need a "double-portion" of God's blessing—that's old school thinking. You've got all the portion you will ever need. It's called Jesus Christ on the inside of you! Even if your faith is as small as a mustard seed, the grace of God makes any breakthrough possible. If it can happen in heaven, it can

> When we fast, we get what God has deposited in us working on the outside.

happen on earth because "He who is in you is greater than he who is in the world" (1 John 4:4). The same power that raised Jesus from the dead is inside of you! You just need to get in alignment so that all that kingdom power in your spirit will manifest itself in your soul and body and in the situations you are facing.

Those things you face in life that might have seemed like a mountain won't seem so big anymore. Your faith will explode and your unbelief will dissipate. When faced with challenges, you will say with confidence, "Mountain, get out of my way!" You will be able to confidently say, just as Paul did, "It is no longer I who live, but Christ lives in me."

Many people have told me, after trying fasting for the first time, that alignment was the first change they noticed. Things get straightened out, life gets back in rhythm, things get fixed and into their rightful place. All of a sudden, there's direction. The fog clears and clarity comes as things start getting aligned properly in their relationships...their jobs...their finances. They sense a peace and order, and realize how misaligned their life had become before they fasted.

> Prayer and fasting should be proactive, not reactive.

Every time I fast, I experience this. I look back with thankfulness to God and think, *What if I hadn't fasted? There is no way I could have gotten into this type of freshness and alignment with God!* So much clear direction. So many miracles happening, but they are all just by-products of aligning my earth with God's heaven.

I want you to think about your life. What challenges are you currently facing or might you face in the future? In order to see God's kingdom come and His will be done, you must be in alignment, and to be in alignment, you must pray and fast.

You may have a problem that seems insurmountable. If we met, you might want to ask me, "Stovall, what about...?"

My answer: "Pray and fast."

"But I think I need—"

"Pray and fast."

"But you don't understand what I—"

"Pray and fast."

"But—"

"Pray and fast."

"Uh…"

"Pray and fast! Pray and fast! Pray and fast! Pray and fast!"

Some things only change when you pray and fast. This is the summary of what Jesus said to the disciples: This kind of _____ (you fill in the blank) will only change, not just when you pray, but when you pray and fast.

You have to be in a greater alignment with God to see certain break-throughs in your life and in the lives of those you love. But when that greater alignment comes, faith arises, unbelief diminishes, and the rule and reign of Jesus can be carried out in our lives. This prepares us to walk in our assignment.

ASSIGNMENT

When we are in agreement and alignment with God, we find that He can use us in ways we never thought possible. We begin walking in our assignment. Now *this* is when the real fun begins! And that is what will bring us the most fulfillment.

What assignment does God have for your life? There is a very specific purpose for which you were created. God is the only One who can truly inform you of that purpose, and in order to fulfill it, you will need His power.

I want you to think about this: Paul and Barnabas were in a season of prayer and fasting with the church in Antioch when the Holy Spirit spoke and gave them their assignment (Acts 13:2–3). Cornelius was in a time of prayer and fasting when he received his assignment (Acts 10:30).

Even Jesus had to receive His assignment. When He was led by the Spirit into the wilderness, He was full of the Holy Spirit (Luke 4:1). This was at the beginning of His ministry, before His assignment. After a forty-day season of prayer and fasting, Jesus came out of the wilderness walking "in the power of the Spirit" (verse 14). Do you see that? He went into the wilderness *full* of the Holy Spirit. He prayed and fasted. Then He came out of the wilderness walking in the *power* of the Spirit.

Going to a deserted place as Jesus did is what fasting represents to us. Remember, fasting is God's way for us to disconnect from the world and its distractions. Symbolically speaking, we depart from the world and go to a deserted place when we fast. It is in this place where we begin to hear the voice of God loud and clear.

> Many of us are full of the Holy Spirit, but we're not walking in the power of the Spirit in the assignment God has for our lives.

Many of us are full of the Holy Spirit, but we're not walking in the power of the Spirit in the assignment God has for our lives. Prayer and fasting will bring that power as we come into agreement and alignment with God. They also help us stay on course with our assignment so that we can steady our focus and not get sidetracked.

Later in this same passage of Scripture, we see that after Jesus had started His public ministry, He was going throughout the region of Galilee and stopped in Capernaum where He did some incredible works. The report in Luke 4:40 says, "When the sun was setting, all those who had any that were sick with various diseases brought them to Him; and He laid His hands on every one of them and healed them."

Can you imagine that? There was a powerful revival going on! But in the middle of all these amazing events, Jesus did something unexpected: "Now when it was day, He [Jesus] departed and went into a deserted place" (verse 42). Even though all all these things were happening, Jesus made it a priority to get alone, in a place of solitude, and tune in to the voice of His Father. "And the crowd sought Him and came to Him, and tried to keep Him from leaving them; but He said to them, 'I must preach the kingdom of God to the other cities also, because for this purpose I have been sent'" (verses 42–43).

Now we must pause and think about this: We just read about all these incredible meetings happening in this town. Unbelievable healings were taking place—God was flat-out on the move. And the crowd was begging Jesus for more. They're like, "Man, Jesus, this is awesome! Let us bring some more of our friends and family members."

Jesus loves people, so I'm sure there was a pull on His heart. The crowd was clamoring for Him, but after tuning in to His Father, Jesus knew what He needed to do. When He came back He basically said, "Sorry guys, I've got to go. These miracles and revivals and all this stuff are great, but this is not the primary purpose for which I have been sent. I must preach the kingdom of God in some other cities too."

Here's the deal: when it comes to pursuing our God-given assignment, if you and I are not in tune with God's voice, we will only hear the voice of the crowd and get weighed down by the pressures of life. This is why fasting is so important: because it clears out all the gunk and the clutter that will drown out God's voice. Like a radio station we can't quite hear clearly, all the voices will cause

> If you and I are not in tune with God's voice, we will only hear the voice of the crowd and get weighed down by the pressures of life.

static and make it difficult for us to tune in to *the* Voice we need to hear.

If we aren't alert, we will confuse God's voice with the voice of the crowd or with other voices like:

- the voice of worry
- the voice of guilt
- the voice of need
- the voice of ambition
- the voice of pressure
- the voice of success
- the voice of failures

Honestly, the voices we hear are not all negative—some of them may be shouting to you about good things. But unless we are tuned in and can hear clearly, we may end up saying yes to the *good* but miss what is *God*. And when you miss what God has in mind, you miss out on your very purpose or assignment.

What might have happened if Jesus had listened to the voice of the crowd? He would have missed His primary purpose and stepped out of the will of His heavenly Father. He would have settled for a very good cause, because those voices were requesting more healing, deliverance, and blessings. But Jesus' primary purpose in His earthly ministry was not to heal diseases and cast out demons but to preach the kingdom of God to lost humanity. Jesus knew that with so much need everywhere, He had to hear the voice of His Father or He would mistakenly choose what's good instead of what's God. That is exactly what will happen in our lives if we're not tuned in to God and hearing His voice over the voice of the crowd.

> We may end up saying yes to the *good* but miss what is *God*.

The voice of the crowd cannot answer the question, "Why are you here?"

When you hear the voice of God, you begin to understand His purpose for you and what you're all about. Then you can prioritize your life around that purpose. That is a freeing place to be, and it uncomplicates your life. Then, you start to understand something foundational about yourself: you're not here on earth simply to exist but—guess what?—you were sent. Your whole life will change when you understand that you were sent here by God.

I don't know what your specific assignment is in regard to your career, relationships, or other matters. I do know that we are all called to be witnesses for Jesus. Every believer is to be a minister of reconciliation (2 Corinthians 5:18–19), bringing people to God the Father to find a relationship with Him. That doesn't mean you are supposed to quit your job and try to work for a church—please don't do that. But what it does mean is that you should look at the normal activities of your everyday life and see them as opportunities to reconcile people to God through Christ. That's a calling for all of us, regardless of our vocation.

Jesus said, "You shall be witnesses to Me" (Acts 1:8). He said not that we are to *go witnessing* but that we are to *be witnesses*. Witnessing is not something we do once a week to fulfill an evangelistic duty. No way! Witnessing should be an overflow of our love for God that spills out onto the people around us.

When we're on fire for God, our lives and our attitudes have an authentic quality of joy and peace that most people are drawn to. When you understand this and have a passion for God and a zeal to be His witness, everything will change as you go to work. You will know God has sent you there for a higher purpose. Whatever your job or business or profession, when you're cutting the deal, making that sale, serving the customer, or whatever you are doing, when you understand that God has sent you to be a witness first, your whole perspective changes. And because of your productivity in the kingdom of God, the blessings will follow. Why wouldn't they? Jesus is the One who said, "Seek first the kingdom of God and His righteousness, and all these things shall be added to you" (Matthew 6:33). You are glorifying God with your life and putting Him first. God wants to equip you with everything you need so that you can have an abundant life, because you're carrying out His assignment.

I can tell you from experience that there's no more exciting way to live than with the understanding that every person you meet during the day, every chance encounter, every trip to Starbucks is actually a potential opportunity to change the course of someone's life and, possibly, the world. What if you are the one who has a part in

> You're not here on earth simply to exist—you were sent here by God.

leading the next Billy Graham to Christ? When you are on fire for God, you can't help but reach out to others. You will give, care, serve, and invite people to church because Christ is in you, living His life.

I understand we can't force God on people. It has to be an overflow of our love for God and a response to the leading of the Holy Spirit. But if you are not on fire for God, you won't light anyone else on fire for God. If you are not happy in God, you won't get anyone else happy in God. This is why having an awakening is so important, and fasting is a key part of that. When we are in agreement and alignment, we will be prepared to handle our assignment from God and the opportunities He puts in front of us.

Agreement. Alignment. Assignment. When these three are operating together in your life, you will be awakened and find yourself experiencing breakthroughs and miracles like never before. You will walk with a sense of purpose you never thought possible!

An Awakening Story

Letting Go of Unbelief

For twelve years I suffered from endometriosis, a painful, incurable disease that affects the female reproductive system. It required several surgeries to help reduce the pain, but inevitably the disease would always grow back within a year or two.

All of my doctors said that I would probably never be able to have children because of the severity of my condition and that my only treatment options were maintenance surgeries and large doses of pain medication.

Just a few days away from my next surgery, my husband and I went to the Friday night prayer meeting that kicked off the Awakening: 21 Days of Prayer and Fasting event at our church. That night Pastor Stovall announced that he really felt like some of us needed to believe for supernatural healing in our bodies. Up until that point, I honestly felt that supernatural healing in the body was only for people of biblical times, or at least only for the "super-spiritual" Christians who have an amazing gift of faith.

As I tried to push these thoughts of unbelief aside and worship, the Holy Spirit began to gently, and then very strongly, convict me of my unbelief, to the point where I could not focus on worship. The Holy Spirit then flooded me with the truth of who God is, His amazing power, and how God yearns for me to believe, *truly believe* that He can do *anything* for His children who love Him.

As I completely surrendered and asked God to give me the faith it required to believe in Him for supernatural things, He began to stir up a faith in me like I had never had before. At the end of the prayer meeting, I had settled in my heart to believe for complete healing of my endometriosis.

Twelve days later I went in for my previously scheduled surgery. My doctor went in to remove all of the diseased tissue and he found none! He didn't know how to explain it, considering what my condition looked like during previous surgeries, which was some of the most aggressive endometriosis doctors had seen in someone my age. All he could say was that he looked everywhere for the endometriosis and all he saw was a very healthy and normal reproductive system—words I had never heard before. I was as ecstatic as you can be coming out of anesthesia and in a little bit of shock and awe at how God moved.

Immediately after the surgery, my husband called David, one of the pastors on staff at Celebration Church, and told him the great news. He told us that the night before that Friday night prayer service, Pastor Stovall had felt the Holy Spirit prompting him to change the sermon he had already prepared for the service. He felt God leading him to speak out of the Gospels, about how Jesus healed the woman who had suffered from bleeding for twelve years. After he had researched what kind of disease this women had, he found that scholars believe she had what we would today call endometriosis!

I was twenty-four at the time of my healing, and just like the woman in the Gospels, Jesus healed me from my issue of bleeding after twelve years. God is so good in how He not only healed me but then gave me that extra confirmation that I had faith.

—DUSTY WILLIAMS

9

Power for Your Willpower

I'M SURE YOU CAN RELATE TO THIS: Have you ever found that there are things you want to do but don't have the willpower to do them? Are there things you say yes to in your heart, but you don't have the strength or energy to follow up with actions? God even may have prompted you to let go of or to distance yourself from some things so you can walk in agreement with Him. But you find yourself not able to follow through on your decision, either because the temptation is too strong or you're easily overcome with fear, weakness, or...you fill in the blank.

All of us have been there, and at one point have felt as if we were losing the battle against our weaknesses or shortcomings. Our willpower was actually lacking of any true power at all! We sometimes reach this point in our walks with God and don't really feel like we have much strength to do the things necessary to keep moving forward in our relationship with Him.

At times we may be able to muster up just enough effort to obey God or be disciplined because we know we should and it's the responsible thing to do. But in all honesty it feels more like an obligation and a "have to." It's like we have to force ourselves into submission, and our response lacks joy and any excitement. We may be doing

> If you don't feel like obeying God, then something is wrong with your feelings.

the right thing, but we are not really following through from a position of spiritual strength and passion. There's a much better way!

Now don't get me wrong; of course, obeying God and exercising discipline regardless of our feelings is the right thing to do and very important. We do have an obligation and responsibility to obey God and live our lives for His glory—even when we don't feel like it. I don't want to diminish that. We reap what we sow, and we will reap good things when we obey God, regardless of how we feel.

Just like we reap benefits and feel better after going to the gym even when we don't really want to, it's still good to go to church when you are not all that jazzed about it. The same goes for reading your Bible, praying, serving, giving, or whatever it is you do for God. In fact, a mark of Christian maturity is when you are able to do the right thing or be disciplined even when you don't feel like it. Typically, the feelings will follow if we take the first step and make an effort to do the right thing.

However, obedience and discipline based on obligation should be the exception, not the norm.

God did not create us to consistently obey Him or walk in spiritual discipline without feeling like it. In fact, if we are obeying out of obligation, this should serve as the first warning sign that it's time to return to our first love (Revelation 2:4–5). Let me put it this way: if you don't feel like obeying God, then something is wrong with your feelings. So much of our Christian teaching focuses on obeying God regardless of how we feel, but the Bible is clear that for the majority of the time we should feel like obeying God. This is where having an awakening comes in. This is where fasting comes in. When you have an awakening with God, you get your feelings back for obeying God and being disciplined. You get strength in your emotions and the power back in your willpower.

Sometimes people get this weird idea that if you do something for God when you really don't want to, it actually makes the action more holy. Bad idea. Is that really the kind of obedience God wants? Are we showing true love for Jesus when His commandments appear burdensome? No, He wants us to do those things because we want to, and because of our affection for Him. Our obedience should be an overflow, a by-product of our love and affection on the inside of us for Jesus. Remember, passionate Christianity is the norm, not the exception. When you are passionate for God and "never… lacking in zeal," you keep your "spiritual fervor" and feel like obeying God (Romans 12:11, NIV). Though we are not led by our feelings, they are important. We are created in the image of God and God created us with emotions and feelings.

Right thinking leads to right feeling. And the way we think right is to renew our minds in the Word of God. When we focus and meditate on the Word of God, understanding what God is truly like and who we are in Christ, which is right thinking, then we have right feeling.

Jesus said, "Take My yoke upon you and learn from Me, for I am gentle and lowly in heart, and you will find rest for your souls. For My yoke is easy and My burden is light" (Matthew 11:29–30). When the feelings that trigger our response to God start to feel burdensome and are not flowing from spiritual strength and affection, this is the first indication of staleness. It means it's time to hit the reset button and get our feelings back for God. The best way to do this is through periodic seasons of prayer and fasting.

> When the feelings that trigger our response to God start to feel burdensome and are not flowing from spiritual strength and affection, this is the first indication of staleness.

One of the first things I discovered when I started fasting over twenty years ago was that fasting motivated me to obey God. I figured out that when I fasted, my body and my actions lined up with what I was saying yes to in my heart. Fasting put the power back in my willpower. It produced within me a fuel for obedience that began to drive my life.

I quickly discovered that within this principle was the key to also releasing God's power in other areas of my life. In addition to obedience and strengthening of my personal relationship with God, fasting also gave me the fuel when it came to any other lifestyle changes that would move me forward in glorifying God even more. Whether it was studying my Bible more, watching less television, eating healthy, working out, spending more quality time with my kids and family, or even setting aside days to rest, fasting fueled my willpower. I had the energy to line my actions up with what I felt God prompting me to do in my heart.

The reason fasting has the potential to do this in such a powerful way is because as we shut down the demands of our flesh and draw closer to God, we release the power of the Holy Spirit living inside of us. It is only through His power that we are able to be and do what God has called us to. It is His power that enables us to live our lives as we should with joy and overcome the fears and obstacles holding us back. Now that's the power we all need fueling our willpower!

When the power of God is in your willpower, you have true power. Prayer and fasting get God's power in your willpower so that the "new man" is alive and the "old man" is dead (Ephesians 4:22–24). The best part is that this fuel is readily accessible to us right now through the power of the Holy Spirit and His Word.

YOU HAVE A WILLING SPIRIT

Jesus warned the disciples (and us too) to "Watch and pray, lest you enter into temptation. The spirit indeed is willing, but the flesh is weak" (Matthew 26:41). I think we often focus on the "flesh is weak" part and skip over the first part of Jesus' statement: "The spirit indeed is willing." In fact many Christians settle into a weak flesh mentality by making a pattern of duty-based obedience and servitude their norm. They end up getting stuck and think they're supposed to feel like that because their "flesh is weak."

Now, while of course it is true that our flesh is weak, we were not intended to live according to the potential of our own strength, or lack thereof. We know our flesh is weak—that's why we need Jesus! So when we're more in tune with that weakness, we need to shift our focus and remember that the spirit is willing. Fasting brings the willingness of our spirit to bear upon our mind, will, and emotions. Fasting allows us to get the power of the Holy Spirit active and working in our thinking and actions again.

"The spirit indeed is willing" means that our new, born-again spirit is willing to do the things that glorify God—and always in a "want to" kind of way. As believers, we know that when we accept Jesus as our Savior, the Holy Spirit comes and dwells inside of us. At that moment, we receive everything we will ever need that pertains to living a life of righteousness or holiness (2 Peter 1:3).

It is that power, the power of the Holy Spirit living within us, that is always persuading us and pointing us Godward. And it is always ready and available to get that same "want to" attitude working in our own actions and feelings. Plus, Jesus didn't say it "might be" willing or sometimes it "will be" willing. No, He said the Spirit "is willing." *All the time.* It never has moments when it doesn't feel like serving or obeying God.

As followers of Christ then, we are settling for much less than God's best and in fact wasting our

> We often focus on the "flesh is weak" part and skip over the first part: "The spirit indeed is willing."

energy when we constantly try to persuade ourselves to do the right thing. The Holy Spirit on the inside of us is already persuading us and encouraging us with joy and strength and power to do all that is needed. When we fast, we release more of that power in our lives and our lifestyle aligns with our spirit's willingness.

When it comes to my devotional time or certain areas of my life, if I start to not feel like obeying God, I know it is time for a fast. Yes, I still obey God when I don't feel like it, but I know that burdensome obedience should be the rare exception, not the norm.

Jesus walked in tremendous power and absolute willingness to obey God. When He was tempted in the wilderness, He completely overcame

Satan's temptations. And notice that this was right after Jesus had prayed and fasted. In fact, He actually described this fuel for obedience that was empowering Him:

> Then Jesus was led up by the Spirit into the wilderness to be tempted by the devil. And when He had fasted forty days and forty nights, afterward He was hungry. Now when the tempter came to Him, he said, "If You are the Son of God, command that these stones become bread." But He answered and said, "It is written, 'Man shall not live by bread alone, but by every word that proceeds from the mouth of God.'" (Matthew 4:1–4)

So what did Jesus mean when He said that "man shall not live by bread alone, but by every word that proceeds from the mouth of God"? Of course He meant that the Word of God is the source of all truth, life, and strength. But it is interesting how Jesus related the Word of God to food. For people to want food, they must be hungry for it.

Food gives us the fuel or energy to live and be healthy. We can relate to that. But what Jesus was saying was that in order to be fueled by the food of His Word, you must first be hungry for it. Although Jesus had a natural appetite and was very hungry for natural bread, He was speaking about His hunger for His true energy source—His spiritual food or fuel. It was this hunger that was driving His decisions and fueling His obedience to His Father. In essence He was saying, "I have a hunger; I have a drive on the inside that natural food cannot satisfy. I live by another type of bread."

Fasting awakens your hunger for God.

In these verses we often focus on the Word of God but forget the hunger component. We understand that we must feed on the Word of God, but in order to do so effectively, we have to be hungry for God. When you are passionate for God, you are hungry for Him. God wants to give you a hunger that only He can satisfy. That is what gives us the power to overcome temptation and obey Him from a consistent "want to" attitude. When you really awaken to this hunger, nothing else will do it for you anymore. Fasting awakens your hunger for God. When you shut down your natural appetite, your spiritual appetite awakens. You are passionate for more of God and your desire for God becomes greater than your other desires.

When it comes to dealing with temptation and sin, I think one of the main problems we run into is that our solution is typically to hold on more tightly to our set of beliefs. We think we just have to try harder and resist more. Now, as Jesus said, of course the Word of God and our belief systems are extremely important. But we should not forget the hunger component. It is this hunger that brings a passion and a desire for God above all other things. This is part of what Jesus was saying in Matthew 4:1–4. We *must* experience hunger for God. Because when it comes to consistently overcoming temptation, our belief systems need to have power behind them. It is actually the hunger for God that will drive the decisions in our lives and enable us to stay faithful to His Word.

Let me explain how this works.

THE SIN EXPERIENCE
VERSUS THE GOD EXPERIENCE

One of the reasons sin is so powerful is that it is an experience. People don't learn about sin; they experience it. And an experience will win over head knowledge every time.

Take my story for example. Before I knew Christ, I was full on into the partying scene. When it came to the cocaine and drinking I did, I didn't just learn about all that stuff—I experienced it. I didn't get into cocaine by studying its molecular structure and how it affected my neural pathways—I experienced its effects. I could not have cared less about the molecules and the chemistry and where the coke came from. I only knew what it made me feel like. It was real to me because I experienced it.

To try and overcome that experience only with a set of beliefs or by learning about God would not have done it for me. In fact, one huge question I had when I was trying to decide if I really wanted to follow God or not was, *Can God really make me feel as good? Can I experience Him like other things in life?* Thank God the answer was a big *yes*! Because the only way I overcame the power of that sin experience was by experiencing God.

When I awakened to God and felt Him, a hunger awakened within me that was so strong, I didn't want to do the sin experience anymore. Sin couldn't satisfy me like God did. But I couldn't just learn about God; I had to experience Him and hunger for Him.

> You cannot overcome a sin experience only with a set of beliefs or by learning about God. You have to *experience* God.

And once I did, everything changed. Because while sin is an experience, God is an even greater experience—the only one that truly satisfies.

The only thing that will truly counter any temptation of the sin experience is the God experience: "No temptation has overtaken you except such as is common to man" (1 Corinthians 10:13). The word *temptation* in this context actually means "a putting to the test of experiences." It gives us the concept of testing two experiences against each other to prove which one is best.

If people are truly experiencing God and His presence, they will choose God over any sin temptation. Because when those experiences are tested against each other, God wins every time. When we "taste and see that the LORD is good" (Psalm 34:8), He fills us with everything we need and we are deeply satisfied. We will hunger not for the sin experience but for God.

The word *overtaken* in the 1 Corinthians passage is not referring to those little everyday miss-the-mark kind of sins we all commit; this is something that has seized you before. It has your number, and it keeps on calling. But even the power of something at this level is diminished when you experience God. The lure of that temptation won't have any power over you, because the

God experience wins over it every time. But without experiencing God in our feelings and in our emotions, which make our experiences authentic, there is no real competition for that sin experience.

This is why it is so important for young people to feel and experience God's presence, not just learn about Him. Youth are all about feelings and experiences. If they can't taste it, feel it, and experience it, then it is not real to them. When they feel and experience life and sin every day and then are told that God is just to be learned about, it is a total disconnect from their reality. But when they truly experience God, He becomes real to them, and He is so much better than the experiences the world is offering them.

> The lure of temptation won't have any power over you, because the God experience wins over it every time.

A great way to do this is to create opportunities for more God experiences in their lives. Get them planted in a local church, share your wisdom and stories with them, and then live the gospel as an example for them to see.

Experiencing God is what true Christianity is all about. Relationships are built on trust and experience. That is what our faith is, a relationship with Jesus. Christianity is a relationship, an experience, a belief system, and a lifestyle all in our Lord and Savior Jesus Christ. You cannot separate these components from one another. They are all intertwined and are crucial to your faith and spiritual growth.

That is what awakening is all about—an immersion in the God experience that becomes a lifestyle. And it is addicting! Fasting brings your God experience and your hunger for God to a whole new level.

God loves to show Himself strong. Give Him a chance to truly compete in the hearts of humanity, and He will provide what nothing else can give us—true love. He will show that only He can truly satisfy.

Experiencing God is the ultimate experience.

An Awakening Story

A Total Life Makeover

In my heart, I always felt as though I was a good person. Yet the circumstances surrounding my childhood had somehow led me to a place I didn't want to be. I grew up around dysfunction, was surrounded by alcoholism, and was molested by a family member when I was about seven years old. That started a pattern that led me to drug use, sexual promiscuity, and abusive behavior, all because I felt I had to prove myself as a young man.

At the age of twelve, I started going to church with my grandparents and a Little League baseball coach. I felt God tugging on my heart, and I responded, accepting Jesus as my Savior, but I didn't quite understand exactly what was going on. I felt the prompting, but didn't actually start living my life for God completely.

Within just a few months, I was hanging out with the wrong crowd, and over the course of the next few years, my life began to slowly fade into a pattern of self-destruction and misery. I lost my chance at a baseball scholarship due to illness, and when that dream ended, I really got into drugs, now even selling things like marijuana, ecstasy, cocaine, pain pills, and others.

I still couldn't see God's goodness in my life, even when my life was spared after being stabbed in the face and throat inches away from my jugular vein. My use of drugs was increasing and became the main focus of my life.

I then met a good friend who invited me to play on a church softball league. I loved sports, so I accepted even though there was tons of craziness going on in my life. During the third season with the team, I remember thinking that here I was playing on this church team for two years, yet I had never set foot in church. I felt a gentle tug from God that I should go.

The only church I ever knew involved singing from hymnals and falling asleep in the pews. But the first time I stepped foot into Celebration Church it was obvious this was different, and I knew it was a place that I could come back to.

I gave my life to the Lord one Sunday while I was actually high in the service. I felt it. I meant it. But I couldn't drop the drugs in my own power. It was such a struggle for me, and I felt myself going back and forth for months, resurrendering my life every couple of weeks, it seemed. I would give my life to the Lord on Sunday and be back to the grind on Monday.

Nonetheless, I kept coming back and even decided to join a singles small group at the church. I started surrounding myself with other Christians. Yet at this point in my life, I was secretly doing OxyContin 24/7, was living with my girlfriend, had a business that was falling apart, was going out drinking nonstop, and yet was still getting into the Word every day. I would stay up high at night studying the Bible. For some reason, I knew there was hope.

Then I heard that we were launching a season of prayer and fasting at the church. All the people from my singles group were participating, so I followed along and tried fasting. I did no drugs that day and ate nothing. I just had juice and water. Then on one of the prayer meeting nights, I remember being in worship with my hands up praising God when Pastor Stovall said, "Can you believe we have been praying for an hour and a half?" I couldn't believe it. It felt like it had only been about fifteen minutes! Then, he asked if anyone wanted to come up and get their prayer language. I had no clue what that was, but I was game for whatever at that point.

I looked up and said to God, "If this is from You, I need You to show me right now." All of a sudden it felt like someone poured a five-gallon bucket of honey over my head that trickled down my whole body. I couldn't move. I experienced God in such a powerful way that night and received my prayer language.

Over the next few weeks, I gained the courage to confess to my small group what I had been struggling with. They prayed for me, and I received my prayer language in full. I haven't touched a drug since.

Many months later, I was helping out with the singles ministry and had been asking God to help me find the right girl. I participated in the very next fast, and the first day, I felt Him reveal who that was—one of the girls I knew in our group. We got engaged behind the cross at the first prayer night and married a week later. We both knew it was a total God thing.

Haley and I got married with one hundred and fifty dollars in our checking account and with sixty thousand dollars in debt. In a year and a half, we paid off twenty-six thousand dollars in debt and had over twenty-eight thousand in the bank. I share this because I was almost bankrupt, but the day I started tithing, my business made a complete turnaround. God continues to bless me and show Himself faithful to His promises.

I hope that someone's life can be changed by my experiences with God. If God could rescue me through all the junk I had in my life, He can rescue anyone.

— SCOTT REVELS

10

No Turning Back

ONCE YOU ARE AWAKENED TO GOD and have the hunger, passion, and freshness back in your relationship with Jesus, it's important to know a few practical principles to keep you from sliding back into some of your former patterns or struggles. Rest assured that when you walk in newfound freedom, the enemy will still be up to his old tricks in trying to pull you back down. Great advice on this is found in the book of Hebrews:

> Seeing then that we have a great High Priest who has passed through the heavens, Jesus the Son of God, let us hold fast our confession. For we do not have a High Priest who cannot sympathize with our weaknesses, but was in all points tempted as we are, yet without sin. Let us therefore come boldly to the throne of grace, that we may obtain mercy and find grace to help in time of need. (4:14–16)

Although Jesus never sinned, He experienced what it was like to have a human body with the same five senses everyone else has. He understands how powerful the voice of temptation can be. I know you are probably thinking, *What do you mean Jesus was tempted at all points like we are? There was no crack back then. There wasn't Internet pornography back then. We have a lot more opportunities for temptation today!* True, there might be different forms of things that tempt us today, but remember that our modern temptations still stem from "the lust of the flesh, the lust of the eyes, and the pride of life" (1 John 2:16). Satan's game plan hasn't really changed. It has gotten some different looks over the years, but it's still the same old stuff.

Thankfully, the Bible also says that "where sin abounded, grace did much more abound" (Romans 5:20, KJV). As long as Jesus is Lord of your life and you want a relationship with Him, it doesn't matter if you've stumbled a hundred times or a thousand times. God loves you and forgives you. He is for you. You will get a breakthrough in your area of struggle after you complete the "Awakening 21-Day Plan" and will enjoy freedom. But God wants you not only to get free but to stay free. He wants you to overcome! Whatever the thing is that used to master you, through the power and grace of God, you can master it!

Let's talk about temptation for a moment and how it comes at us. There are two scriptures I want to unpack. In studying these two together, we find some key principles in getting free and staying free.

First, in James 1:14 we see that temptation actually starts way before the act of sin takes place itself: "But each one is tempted when he is drawn away by his own desires." So before the act of sin, a drawing away takes place.

Next, let's look at 1 Corinthians 10:12–13:

> Therefore let him who thinks he stands take heed lest he fall. No temptation has overtaken you except such as is common to man; but God is faithful, who will not allow you to be tempted beyond what you are able, but with the temptation will also make the way of escape, that you may be able to bear it.

So here we see that we can actually choose the way of escape, and in James 1:14, we see the temptation starts when you are drawn away by your own desires. Incidentally, this is exactly why your desire (passion) for God needs to be above all other desires. Awakening takes your passion and desire for God above all other desires so you have your freedom back and your power to choose. So choose well! Make the right decisions and choices that line up with God's Word and commit to those. By doing this you are choosing the way of escape referred to in 1 Corinthians 10:13 before the opportunity to sin even presents itself.

This leads us to another key principle: we can choose our way of escape well before the temptation is unbearable. Remember, once you complete the "Awakening 21-Day Plan," you will have both your hunger for God and your willpower back. You will be in a strong spiritual state to choose well, make some positive decisions, and set some healthy boundaries that you can manage in the future.

You will stay spiritually strong if you decide what is the right thing to do according to the Word of God and then manage that decision for the rest of your life. Once you do that, regardless of the season of life or the circumstance you are in, or even if you hit a moment of weakness, you can protect yourself. You shouldn't re-decide things according to the moment. You decide one time and then manage that decision.

> We can choose our way of escape well before the temptation is unbearable.

This is like deciding that you are going to be passionate for God and embrace a lifestyle of devotions and fasting. You decide one time and then manage that decision for the rest of your life. Or you decide that being faithful to a local church is the right thing to do, and you manage that decision for the rest of your life.

This is also the first step when it comes to staying free and overcoming temptation. The Bible says that God will provide a "way of escape." But God's way of escape starts with the decisions and boundaries we put in place before the opportunity to sin even presents itself. When you are free and strong spiritually, that is the time to make the decision and put those boundaries in place, if they are not already there, and commit to them.

Think about how this principle already operates in your life. Hopefully, you don't wake up every morning and think, *I wonder if I should go to work today. Let's see… What's on TV? What else might I want to do instead of going to work? Maybe I'll stay home.* Of course you don't do that. You decide one time when you get your job that you're going to go to work every day. Imagine how unproductive (and unemployed) you'd be otherwise! You decide one time and then you manage that decision. It doesn't matter how nice the weather is that day or what other opportunities come your way, or what your friends are doing. You have a job, so you go to work. Case closed.

Now take that same principle and apply it to temptation. Let's say you're trying to get out of a party lifestyle, and you're fired up for God and doing great. One of your friends invites you and a few buddies to a bar and grill–type place after work. You go, but then at that bar you're invited to have a couple of beers at a nightclub. So you innocently go there and plan on having just one beer, but you end up having three beers and before long someone invites you to their house for a later party. Many of your co-workers are going, so you go and plan on stopping by for a few minutes. You get over there and it ends up being way more than just a party. You stay late, and then after most people have left, the drugs come out. Now what do you do? It's time to pray. Probably something like this: "God, give me the way of escape! Get me out of this! I have been doing great, but now this is hard to resist."

News flash! Your way of escape was not at your third party when the drugs got dumped out on the coffee table. Your way of escape was when you were invited for a few beers at that nightclub. You should have said, "No thanks" then, knowing that the next stop could set you up for temptation.

Being awakened and hungry for God doesn't mean you should push the limits with your freedom. We will always be susceptible to temptation. Jesus illustrated this in the wilderness when even after He had already rebuked Satan twice, His next comment was, "You shall not tempt the LORD your God" (Luke 4:12). Even though you are passionate about God and driven by hunger for Him, don't think you can push the envelope and are no longer susceptible to temptation. As long as you live in a human body, the spirit will be willing but the flesh weak (Mark 14:38). Choosing the way of escape must be done before the opportunity fully presents itself.

Let's take pornography as another example. If this is your issue, then a way of escape is not to be first sought when you're already in your room by yourself one click away from the wrong Web site. The way of escape is to get an Internet filter on your computer, move that machine to a public room in the house, and get in a group or have a friend whom you can be open with and become accountable in that area.

If your issue is sexual purity in a dating relationship, your way of escape will probably not present itself when you are alone, making out in a dark bedroom at 2:00 a.m. Do you see what I'm saying? The way of escape came around midnight when you brought her home after your date and saw her roommate wasn't there. (Hint: Say goodnight at the door.) To find your way of escape you have to decide ahead of time what your boundaries are going to be.

One of the biggest mistakes we make is when we allow ourselves to walk alongside the edge of temptation. It's really like walking along the edge of a cliff; all it takes

> Choosing the way of escape must be done before the opportunity fully presents itself.

is one little wind gust to blow us over. But we keep walking on the edge of the cliff, looking over the edge and praying, "God help me." And God is saying, "Get away from the edge of the cliff, genius! You shouldn't even be on that side of the mountain. Come back over here and walk alongside Me."

BE WATCHFUL AND ENDURE

Jesus said, "Watch and pray, lest you enter into temptation" (Mark 14:38). He didn't just say "pray" about temptation; He said "watch." Watch for the way of escape. Make the decision to set whatever boundaries you need to put in place. This will put you in a position to stay free and able to endure when the temptation comes for you to violate those boundaries.

God will give you the power to stay faithful to those boundaries and decisions you have made when you are tempted to violate them. And you will be rewarded for enduring the temptation. James 1:12 says, "Blessed is the man who endures temptation; for when he has been approved, he will receive the crown of life which the Lord has promised to those who love him."

Through an awakening with God and making the right decisions, you will overcome and He'll give you the crown of life. A literal fulfillment of this verse will occur in heaven where we will get crowns and cast them at Jesus' feet. But there is also a present fulfillment.

Think about it: A crown represents authority. Kings wear crowns because they are in charge. That is why Jesus will be crowned with many crowns (Revelation 19:12). He has all authority.

> You will come into a new level of spiritual authority when you overcome temptation.

One of the things James 1:12 is saying is that you will come into a new level of spiritual authority when you overcome temptation. By the grace of God, you will master the thing that once mastered you and exchange the death that it used to bring to you for the life of God. But the key is your passion for God. Having the God experience breaks the strength of the sin experience. To put it simply, you will be more passionate about God than you are about sin. You won't want to mess up your God high with some cheap substitute that doesn't satisfy.

Through the "Awakening 21-Day Plan," not only will you get free, but you will stay free if you decide ahead of time to choose the way of escape.

An Awakening Story

Rescued by God's Love

When I moved to Jacksonville, Florida, I was in a place of emotional brokenness. I was five months pregnant, and everything I owned was in the back of my car. I had just walked away from a relationship of seven years that had failed due to our crazy lifestyle. He was a street racer and I was a bartender.

I struggled with alcohol and felt as if my value came from my looks. Every bad choice I had ever made brought me to where I was. I had an incurable STD and no self-esteem, and I now had to start my life over as a single mom. I felt as if I had ruined my life, and all I could wonder was how I had gotten to this point.

In my car on the way to Jacksonville, I told God to have His way in my life. I told Him I would do whatever He wanted me to do. I just knew I desperately needed a fresh start.

My first weekend in Jacksonville, I attended Celebration Church and my life hasn't been the same since. Shortly thereafter, I heard announced that the Awakening: 21 Days of Prayer and Fasting was starting. Even though I was pregnant, I still wanted to participate in the fast somehow. So I decided to fast from the secular music I had listened to all my life. Instead, I listened to sermons and some worship music my sister had given me. I must have listened to the same five songs over and over throughout the fast.

On the last prayer night ending the fast, I went to the altar and asked for God to have favor on me and heal my STD. I can proudly say that my body has been completely healed, I have been sexually pure, and I will remain so until I am married.

The fast changed my life and laid the foundation for my relationship with Christ. I didn't even know it then, but secular music had a stronghold on one of the very areas I was created for. After the fast, I didn't even want to go back to listening to the same music I had listened to. I threw away over two hundred and fifty CDs at my church small group, and now I serve on the worship team, leading others to experience the presence of God in worship!

Prayer and fasting have become a part of my walk with God. God's love for me is evident in my life and His love story to rescue me is something I will never forget. I love my life, love being a mom, enjoy being a part of the body of Christ, serve gladly on the worship team, fully trust God as my provider, and tithe 10 percent.

Above all, I know that I am loved and have value in the eyes of Jesus Christ who died for me.

—CASSIA WERN

11

Fasting for Your Health

The best of all medicines is resting and fasting.
—BENJAMIN FRANKLIN

THE PHYSICAL BENEFITS OF FASTING are widely known. I admit that losing weight is a natural benefit to fasting, and it's one that many, including myself, are fine with receiving. I've also known physicians who recommend fasting for medical reasons, and that's completely understandable, as fasting has tremendous health benefits for your physical body. There are now even clinics in America where people go to fast for medical reasons. In addition to the spiritual benefits, there is absolutely nothing wrong with fasting as a prescription for health.

Up front let me say that, obviously, I am not a medical professional. The information I'm sharing with you here regarding physical benefits of fasting is what I have found mainly through personal experience. Before you make fasting a regular spiritual discipline, I encourage you to make an appointment with your family physician to discuss a personalized fasting plan. Your doctor will know your medical history and will advise you not only if you should fast but how you should fast.

One of the primary physical benefits of fasting that I've found is that very much like our souls, when we fast, our bodies reset themselves. Quite simply, our bodies need to rest from time to time, and fasting is one of the best ways we can do that. Even those who take reasonably good care of their physical health with proper diet and regular exercise can benefit from hitting the reset button physically through fasting from time to time.

In addition to the spiritual benefits of fasting, the Bible also mentions many of the physical benefits as well. Let's look at Isaiah 58:

Is this not the fast that I have chosen:
To loose the bonds of wickedness,
To undo the heavy burdens,
To let the oppressed go free,
And that you break every yoke?
Is it not to share your bread with the hungry,
And that you bring to your house the poor who are cast out;
When you see the naked, that you cover him,
And not hide yourself from your own flesh?
Then your light shall break forth like the morning,
Your healing shall spring forth speedily,
And your righteousness shall go before you;
The glory of the LORD shall be your rear guard.
Then you shall call, and the LORD will answer;
You shall cry, and He will say, "Here I am." (verses 6–9)

In this passage God speaks about freedom from sin, addictions, and oppression (verse 6). He also mentions what that inner freedom is going to produce—a passion to serve others (verse 7). Did you notice the awakening principle there? You have to get freed up and passionate for God before you can truly free somebody else! And then God speaks about healing and righteousness (verse 8). He is referring not only to spiritual healing but to physical healing and freshness, which fasting brings to the body.

God designed fasting to be a healing medicine all by itself. There are some great books in your health food store on all the health benefits of fasting. I encourage you to read one during your twenty-one-day fast. Reading about the cleansing, detoxifying, and healing taking place inside your body while you fast will help keep you motivated.

In his informational book *Juice Fasting and Detoxification*, Steve Meyerowitz gives a great, concise picture of the healing done in the body during a fast: "When you fast, you are on nature's operating table. The body changes hats. Instead of being in the business of receiving, processing, storing, analyzing, assimilating, discriminating and discarding, it shifts to the job of house cleaning, removal, sanitizing, refurbishing and renewal. It is a big job and it is not without its inconveniences, especially when there is someone living in the house."*

> God designed fasting to be a healing medicine all by itself.

That may sound as if our body is a manufacturing plant running around the clock, which is an accurate description. The body is receiving, processing, storing, analyzing, assimilating, discriminating, and discarding food. Wow! That is a lot of work—no wonder we are tired so often. Eating may be a great pleasure, but it's also serious work. Our body constantly works overtime to digest and assimilate all that food, especially when it is processed food full of sugar and salt, like much of the American diet is. Our stomach, liver, and kidneys never get a chance to rest and rejuvenate, unless we fast and give them a much-needed break.

When we fast, the blood and energy that is constantly in use to help digest food can finally go to help rejuvenate other parts of our body, such as the brain. This is why it is very common to experience what I call a fast fog for about the first seven days of your fast. But after day eight or so, you will feel like someone has cleaned your brain out. Your thinking clears after your body flushes out all those toxins. Your tongue will probably even have a white film on it. Seriously, check it out. I know that might sound pretty gross, but just think—that is all the gunk coming out of your body!

The first thing your body wants to do when you fast is attack and

---

* Steve Meyerowitz, *Juice Fasting and Detoxification* (Great Barrington, MA: Sproutman, 1999), 73.

remove the impurities and toxins. This may also cause you to feel a little achy and maybe even a little weak for the first seven days as your body adjusts, but after that most people feel light and energized. Be encouraged—the aches, weakness, and fogs are a good thing and are only temporary. In my experience, I am feeling so much of the presence of God that I don't even care!

Just like our souls, the inside of our bodies needs a good spring cleaning from time to time. Once you get a good scrub, you will notice your body beginning to crave it from time to time, as if saying, "Please, give me a break. Let me rest. Let me clean up. Stop stuffing garbage in me for just a few days so I can recover!"

> Fasting is a simple process of cleaning house.

The physical benefits of fasting can be summarized with these words: house cleaning, removal, sanitizing, refurbishing, and renewal. Fasting is a simple process of cleaning house, getting rid of the garbage that has accumulated—maybe for years. We do not need special medicines to do this; God created our bodies to do the job naturally.

While you fast, not only are you burning fat cells, but you are also cleansing toxins stored in your body's fat. This is why fasting is one of the greatest and healthiest ways to lose weight. And it is actually easier to keep the weight off when you resume a normal healthy diet because your cells are cleansed.

Can fasting even one day a week do all that? Or do you need to go on an extended fast for those benefits? Let's look more closely at what fasting does to restore us physically.

Your car is a great illustration of the effects of fasting, especially if you drive a minivan and have young kids. Have you ever found that you can spend more time in your car than in your house? It can get to the point where it feels as if you are living out of your car, driving your kids everywhere: off to school in the morning, and then all the after-school activities, birthday parties, soccer games, dance recitals, church, Starbucks stops, fast-food restaurants, the grocery store, and, finally, back home. Whew, but then you start all over again the next day.

After a while, all of those hamburger wrappers, the uneaten fries, the empty juice boxes, gum wrappers, and other gunk pile up. Then your car starts to smell (especially if you have a baby who has thrown a few milk bottles under the seat!). You get to the point where you can't take it anymore and, finally, one Saturday you get the vacuum and all your cleaning stuff and nuke that sucker with an atomic cleaning bomb. *Yes!* And it feels so good to have the family bus clean and sanitized.

Over time, many of us can start to feel like that trashed van. We're all gunked-up and in desperate need of a deep cleaning. We didn't do this intentionally; it just happened. Like with the minivan, after so much use and everyday life, garbage builds up. Likewise, our bodies are driven non-stop. It's time for a good cleaning, so don't do it halfway. Use the atomic cleaning bomb of fasting!

Cleaning, whether it's your home, car, body, or anything else, not only is a vital way to keep things operating correctly but also helps them last longer.

The human body is like a pack rat; it can hold on to things that really should be thrown away. If not cleansed from time to time, it will hold on to

> The human body is like a pack rat; it can hold on to things that really should be thrown away.

extra fat, water, and—how do I say this politely?—waste. It tucks these extras into nooks and crannies in our bodies where they cannot be properly eliminated. As gross as this may sound, these extras can stay in your body for months, even years. And this is not a good thing.

When you fast, however, the body does not have its usual energy source of food so it must use stored fat cells. When these reserve fat cells are burned, fatty acids that have accumulated are also released and eliminated through the colon, kidneys, lungs, and skin. Toxins—poisons—that have been trapped in these reserve cells are now freed, and the body discards them as trash.

This is why when you fast, especially when you fast for longer than twenty-four hours, you may develop bad breath or body odor. While unpleasant, it is the body's natural way of getting rid of what should not have been stored in the first place.

There are other kinds of cells in your body—dead or dying cells—that fasting treats harshly, which is also a very good thing. When energy is not readily present for these cells, they turn on themselves in a process called autolysis. Thus, through fasting the body rids itself of unhealthy cells.

When you are eating, your body uses much of its energy to digest food. So when you are fasting, extra energy is freed up and available to rejuvenate the senses. Areas of your physical being that are used day after day (the minivan analogy) get worn out and need to be refreshed. When you fast, the body has the time and the materials to refresh your taste buds, your sense of smell, your eyesight, and your hearing. I have noticed that even my sinuses feel cleared, allowing me to breathe more easily. It is as if your body is a giant computer that starts to freeze up and fasting is the reboot button.

> It is as if your body is a giant computer that starts to freeze up and fasting is the reboot button.

I'm always amazed at how good food tastes after a fast. Even whole-grain bread is wonderful. Although I might eat turkey wraps all the time, for example, after an extended fast it tastes like I am eating that wrap for the first time!

If you are planning to change your diet—not go on a diet, but change your eating patterns as a means of establishing a healthier lifestyle—know that it is very common for people to experience a long period of discomfort as their bodies adapt to the new nutritional plan. But if they fast before beginning the new dietary plan, these symptoms can be reduced or even eliminated. And if there are any physical addictions, including alcohol, tobacco, or drugs, a time of fasting can help to break these addictions.

We see this happen over and over in our church. People come and surrender to Christ, and then the first time they go on a fast like during Awakening, they are set free from a physical addiction. Of course, there's a huge spiritual component to this as well. Much of this book is about the spiritual power of fasting and prayer, and it is God who truly sets a person free. But the same power you use when you say no to food during a fast is available to say no to drugs or any other addiction. If you say no to food, you will be surprised what else you can say no to. Remember, fasting gets the power back in your willpower.

Additional physical benefits of fasting include:

- increased energy
- better and deeper sleep patterns
- clearer skin
- mental and emotional recharging
- stronger resistance to illness
- more self-control

Fasting does require reasonable precautions. There are situations that make it advisable for some people not to fast, or at least not until receiving approval from a physician. If you have any health concerns, please consult your physician prior to beginning your fast—especially if you are taking medication, have a chronic condition, or are pregnant or nursing.

Sometimes when family and friends find out that you are going on a twenty-one-day fast, they worry and get concerned about your health. In fact, as you have read this book, you might have become a little worried yourself. Let me assure you that, done with your doctor's permission, fasting is one of the best things you can do for your body.

Do not delay giving your body the rest and restoration it so deserves.

An Awakening Story

Miracle Baby

We started attending Celebration Church in December 2006. We had been through a lot the previous two years having had four miscarriages after having our son. Our faith had been tested beyond all measure, and we just needed a good place to call our church home. We immediately knew that Celebration Church was the place for us.

We had decided to try to have a baby one more time, and if I miscarried again then that would be it for us.

We learned about the fasting and prayer in January and we decided to participate. We fasted and then came to the prayer service at the end of the fast. Pastor Stovall called people to the altar for healing. We went down to get prayer for God to heal me and allow me to have another child.

On February 12, I found out I was pregnant. On October 15, I gave birth to a beautiful baby girl. As I type this, I am holding her in my arms. She is a miracle, and I want to praise God for what He has done. There were so many people and ministries praying for us during this time, and I praise God for all of them.

— STEPHANIE BRUNK

12

The Awakening Story

SOON AFTER I BECAME A CHRISTIAN I heard a message on fasting and it made total sense to me, just like Bible reading and prayer. The church I attended at the time had a forty-day period of fasting every year. From the first time I experienced it, I made fasting a part of my lifestyle and treated it with the same value as I do my personal devotion time with God. I am so thankful for this, because it is this lifestyle of prayer, fasting, and personal devotion that has shaped me as a Christian.

I have been fasting regularly for over twenty years now, and I could tell you countless stories of the impact it has had not only in my personal life but also in Celebration Church. Through these times of seeking God and drawing closer to Him, I've experienced many amazing miracles and breakthroughs. I have also received some of the most precise, specific direction for my own life, my family, and our church. Without fail, each time I fast I look back in amazement at what God has done in my heart and what He has revealed to me and I wonder, *Man, what if I wouldn't have fasted? I would have totally missed out on what God had for me and our church.* Most of which has led us to where we are today as a church.

> Each time I fast I look back in amazement at what God has done in my heart and what He has revealed to me.

It amazes me that, at the time of writing this book, our church is nearly twelve years old. When God called my wife, Kerri, and me to Jacksonville to start Celebration Church, we began from scratch—literally with nothing. Our launch team was a group of seven people. We held services in a gym and were mobile for the first few years. Oh the stories I could share!

Our church has experienced incredible spiritual and numerical growth. We have seen thousands of individuals come to Christ for the first time, and we currently have an attendance of more than ten thousand people each week. We have enjoyed amazing favor while expanding both regionally and internationally. Celebration Church is now a global, multisite church with twelve campuses.

> There is something so powerful about setting aside time at the start of each new year to pray, fast, and seek God.

We have seen amazing moves of God and are leading people to experience the God-first life. Through all of our weekend and extension services, we witness hundreds of people make decisions for Christ every single week. And to think it all started with a group of seven people meeting in a gym! When people see what God is doing in and through Celebration Church, they often ask what's the greatest contributing factor to this growth and the passion, energy, and hunger for God that exude from our church and staff. While great leadership, services, ministry, programs, and systems are crucial in moving the church forward, quite simply the answer is that our church was built on seeking God. At the end of the day, all else aside, we are a church that prays, fasts, and seeks God, and we always will be. And for that, there is no substitute.

This is more than a program for us. It is now embedded deep in our culture. We have been able to share this same emphasis of prayer and fasting with hundreds of other pastors, churches, and ministry leaders around the world through Awakening: 21 Days of Prayer and Fasting.

Since the church began, our staff has always fasted at the beginning of the year. But six years ago, I felt God prompting me to introduce a twenty-one-day season of prayer and fasting to our Celebration Church leadership and key volunteers. This has been a personal practice of mine each January for years. There is something so powerful about setting aside time at the start of each new year to pray, fast, and seek God.

The results with leadership were incredible, and the spiritual momentum flooded out into our church. It was amazing how much clarity and alignment God brought to our plans for the year. The fast literally jump-started our year.

After seeing what this had done in our staff and leadership, I felt God tell me it was time to roll it out to our church. We did so the very next January, and Celebration Church has never been the same since.

What I saw was that the people in our church were not only willing, but hungry to participate in this powerful experience of drawing closer to God. They just needed to be led and given the tools. This is one of the common misconceptions I hear from other pastors about fasting. Their concern is that introducing fasting to their congregation will push people away, especially the unchurched and people who don't have a relationship with God yet. But we have found that not to be true. In fact, we've seen the opposite.

We've actually seen God using an unbeliever's fast as the catalyst that draws that person into an authentic relationship with Jesus. We've seen people who were far away from God try fasting for the first time, and then awaken to the presence of God like never before. We simply should not draw our own conclusions based out of fear or lack of understanding and close the door on such a beneficial experience. Fasting for health and weight loss is very popular in the secular world right now, and unchurched people neither fear it nor think it to be extreme. Fasting is a spiritual discipline God designed for us, and fruit always comes from it.

So we rolled out the first twenty-one-day fast to Celebration Church and quickly pulled some basic resources together. We encouraged the people in our church to think about the one or two top things on their hearts that they wanted to pray about. That month, I preached an entire message series on the

benefits of fasting, and they identified with the newness they
...eeded and wanted to feel in their souls.

Every year since then, we have seen more people saved, passion for Jesus,
personal breakthroughs, miracles, and people drawing closer to God than
ever before. We find our church actually looks forward with great anticipation to Awakening each January. It has been satisfying to see the spiritual
growth and awesome miracles that people experience.

> When you have a culture of prayer
> and fasting, you see a sustained
> freshness and newness in people's
> relationship with God.

A few years ago, one
of my good friends, Dino
Rizzo, who pastors Heal-
ing Place Church, an in-
credible, thriving church
in Baton Rouge, told me
we should open this sea-
son of prayer and fasting up to other churches to participate with us. He said
we should use what we had learned and our resources to help equip the body
of Christ at large. "Let's all do this together and have a great kingdom impact," he urged. I wasn't sure exactly how that would work, but I knew what
it would do for other churches and believers if they could just experience
what we had experienced.

I believe fasting is one of those things that should be periodically done
together; in other words, corporately. After experiencing it and being so passionate about the results of prayer and fasting in my personal life, and then
seeing the impact it made in our staff and leadership and then in our church,
we opened it up to the body of Christ and launched Awakening: 21 Days of
Prayer and Fasting.

There are great churches around the globe that start every year with
prayer and fasting and have even been doing it a lot longer than we have.
There are other churches that have never tried it but want to. By uniting with
these churches and providing fasting resources and tools, we want to help
churches develop cultures of prayer and fasting in their congregations.

I think at times a church may pray and fast for a big event or cause or outreach, but it is another thing entirely to develop a culture of prayer and fasting. When you have a culture of prayer and fasting, you see a sustained freshness and newness in people's relationship with God, as well as throughout each ministry area and the church as a whole.

The very first year we opened up Awakening to the body of Christ, 364 pastors, churches, and ministries participated. This represented around 350,000 people. It was great! Many of them were fasting for the first time, so they experienced the results for the first time as well. The testimonies streamed in, telling of fasting-related events like those we've experienced at Celebration Church. Marriages were being restored, physical healings were taking place, and people were awakening to the presence of God in powerful ways as alignment occurred in their lives and ministries.

The next year, in January 2010, the number grew to 1,086—that's nearly eleven hundred pastors, churches, and ministries around the world praying and fasting together at the onset of the year. This represented over one million believers!

The most consistent feedback we've received from participating churches is that they've experienced a tremendous increase in salvations and baptisms, as well as an increased level of individual participation in small groups, serving, and giving. This is what happens when people awaken to God. All these things go to the next level because people are passionate and hungry for God. They get that "want to" attitude back, and it begins driving their life. The spiritual vitality of the church then rises to the next level. Many church plants attributed a successful launch to prayer and fasting. Because leaders and members were so in tune with God, things took off quickly and the ministry thrived. I could go on and on. Once you experience it—there's just no going back.

A WORD FOR PASTORS AND MINISTRY LEADERS

If you have a desire to establish a culture of prayer and fasting in your church or ministry, I want to encourage you to try a corporate fast. Your ministry will never be the same. A great way to get started is to join us in January for Awakening: 21 Days of Prayer and Fasting. Register your church or ministry online at www.awake21.org, and pray and fast together with the hundreds of other pastors, churches, and ministries all around the world that are a part of this each January. As we harness the power of doing this together, you can literally feel the momentum propelling us forward together.

Choose whatever those twenty-one days will look like for your church. There are several resources, tips, and tools available at www.awake21.org that you can use. You may choose to participate for all of the twenty-one days or even simply one day a week. Should the selected dates for the twenty-one-day season need to be adjusted to fit your ministry planning calendar, that's up to you. The primary goal is that we all set aside some time at the beginning of the year to pray and fast together for the advancement of God's kingdom.

As a registered pastor or church leader, you will have access to use any of the free fasting resources available at www.awake21.org. Some of these include:

- fasting message series including videos, downloads, message transcripts, and sermon notes
- informational videos on how to establish a culture of prayer and fasting in your church
- practical information on prayer and fasting that includes a list of different types of fasts, fasting instructions, a fasting calendar, and more
- a twenty-one-day devotional
- fasting ideas for kids
- the Awakening youth fasting guide
- Awakening branding, media, and graphics

Whether you've fasted before or if this would be your first time, I hope you'll join us. There's something so powerful about setting aside this time at the beginning of the year to pray, fast, and seek God together. I know what it has done in my life and in our church. I can't wait to see what it will do in yours!

INDIVIDUAL PARTICIPATION

I want to also invite individuals to join together with the million-plus people around the world who participate in Awakening each year. Follow the "Awakening 21-Day Plan" provided in this book and log on to our Web site at www.awake21.org to find out more. We want to know that we are praying and fasting with you as well, so be sure to register and let us know how we can pray for you.

> This will be your best year ever, if it is your best year *spiritually*.

Let me say again, this will be your best year ever, if it is your best year *spiritually*. And as you pray, fast, and draw closer to Him, get ready for incredible things to start taking place in your life!

An Awakening Story

Miracle Babies

Jennifer, our youngest daughter, is much like her mother in that she has always had strong maternal instincts. She's always wanted to be a mother. About a year after she and her husband, Ben, were married, they found out they were expecting a child. Amid the excitement of choosing names, painting a nursery, and all of the accompanying joys of planning for that first baby, the doctor told them the pregnancy was tubal. After much agonizing in prayer, the pregnancy ended, resulting in the loss of the baby and damage to the fallopian tube, making further pregnancies less likely. Following a period of grieving, Ben and Jenny decided to try again. After a few months she became pregnant and the anticipation began anew. Our hearts were broken, however, when we discovered that this was also a tubal pregnancy, now on the other side. The story played out with similar results—no baby and too much damage done to the other fallopian tube to support future pregnancies.

As a family we prayed through our options: to accept this as being the will of God and have Ben and Jenny continue to pour their lives into other people's children, to explore adoption, or to investigate the possibility of in vitro fertilization. They decided on the latter, carefully treating the fertilized eggs as gifts from God. Again, hopes were raised, only to be dashed when the call came that the procedure did not take.

As parents, we grieved with our daughter and son-in-law, feeling their pain deeply every time one of Jenny's siblings would announce an impending pregnancy. She was so brave in rejoicing with them, but we knew that her heart was breaking with the desire to be a mother.

They decided to try one more time. It happened to coincide with our church's joining Celebration Church in the twenty-one days of fasting at the beginning of the year. My wife and I decided to make Ben and Jenny the focus of our prayers during this time. Our custom was to light candles as an expression of intercessory prayer at the conclusion of our services, so Debbie and I would quietly do so together, asking God to bless their home with a child in spite of the medical evidence to the contrary.

As a church, we celebrated the end of the fast with a worship service on the first Wednesday in February. The next morning Ben and Jenny received word that they would soon become the parents of not one but two new babies. A little less than eight months later we welcomed our miracle baby girls, Rylan Hope and Sadie Joy Mayer into our family. God gave Ben and Jenny the *hope* of becoming parents, and *joy* is how they feel every time they look at the girls, knowing what they've been through to get them here.

Needless to say, the Awakening 21 Days of Prayer and Fasting has taken on a new level of meaning in the Surratt household. We are once again reminded that nothing is impossible with God.

—GREG SURRATT, LEAD PASTOR OF SEACOAST CHURCH

THE AWAKENING
21-DAY PLAN

D EAR READER,

I am so glad you've decided to participate in an extended time of fasting and prayer! I can assure you that this will be an experience like no other. I have found that there is no better way to reset my spiritual compass and bring about refreshing in every area of my life than through prayer and fasting.

The "Awakening 21-Day Plan" is flexibly designed so that you can participate at any level. Whether you have done a twenty-one-day season of prayer and fasting before or if this is your first time, you can start where you are and experience what God has in store for you in a powerful way.

The tools provided in this section are a practical guideline to help you navigate through your personal twenty-one-day plan. As you read over the information, consider how it applies to your personal circumstances and convictions.

Your twenty-one-day plan is designed to walk you through the daily practice of the key topics we've discussed in this book:

- experiencing surrender
- experiencing passion for God

- experiencing God's goodness
- creating space for God to fill

Every installment of the twenty-one-day plan includes these features: devotional, "Bible Reading Plan," "Prayer Focus," and "The Awakening Journey"—a place for you to record your thoughts as your fast progresses. There's also the "Optional Book Reading Plan" that will guide you through a complete reading of *Awakening* during the twenty-one days. And, finally, if you would like to gather with friends for support and fellowship during the twenty-one-day experience, I have included a three-session "Small Group Study Guide" for your use.

I assure you, this will be your best year ever if it is your best year *spiritually*. I pray that you will experience the presence and power of God in an extraordinary way as you commit yourself to Him over the next twenty-one days. May God continue to bless you and enlarge you as you seek Him first!

Stovall Weems

WHY TWENTY-ONE DAYS?

Awakening is a lifestyle, and learning how to incorporate the principles we've discussed into your everyday life is easy and sustainable. I've found that when people pray and read their Bibles for twenty-one days in a row, as with most activities done continually for that long, it becomes a habit. And when people experience the power of a twenty-one-day fast, it easily becomes a natural part of their lives.

WHAT YOU'LL NEED

In addition to the tools provided in this twenty-one-day plan, you will need a Bible. Most of the Scripture references I have used in this book are from the New King James Version, but it's important that you find a translation that works for you. The New International Version and the New Living Translation are also great and easy to read.

In addition, I recommend the use of a personal journal, which will help you capture and record all of the incredible things God is speaking into your life. Having your personal preference of worship music readily available on a CD or on your iPod is a great idea as well. And of course, depending on the type of fast you choose to follow, some preparation is required, too. I will be discussing this in the section on fasting.

I also recommend having a scratch pad available. This is for writing down all those annoying things that will creep in while you're trying to focus on God's voice. Use the scratch pad to make a to-do list of things to accomplish later so that you can get them out of your mind during this time devoted to God.

Lastly, you need to choose a place and time. Prayer, Bible reading, and personal devotions are foundational parts of this plan. Choosing a spot and even a specific place where you will seek God every day is so important, whether this means getting up thirty minutes earlier in the morning or finding some quiet space in your car on your lunch break. If you know where and when you plan to meet God, you are more likely to show up. He will certainly be there waiting for you!

PRAYER

Your twenty-one-day plan will include prayer as a key part of your daily practice. As you prepare for the next twenty-one days, it can be tempting to start thinking of a laundry list of prayers you'd love to see answered. But I encourage you to keep this simple. Think about the top two or three things most pressing on your heart and zone in on those with God. Write these in your journal and be open to hearing what He wants to show you in those areas. Remember, the breakthroughs, miracles, and answers to your prayers will be by-products of drawing closer to Jesus.

When praying, make your primary goal to know Jesus more and experience Him. Remember to focus on the goodness, greatness, and glory of God. Pray prayers of total surrender, and aim to glorify God with your life. Focus first on what's right about Him and see everything else through that filter.

> When praying, make your primary goal to know Jesus more and experience Him.

And most simply, make time to pray daily. Don't overcomplicate this! Just talk to God. Have that place and time where you can seek Him every day. If you don't plan to pray, you won't. If you find it a challenge to disconnect from the busyness of your day, engaging in worship music is a great way to prepare your heart for prayer.

PERSONAL DEVOTIONS

A primary aspect of the awakening lifestyle that produces spiritual growth is spending time in God's Word. In addition to daily prayer, your twenty-one-day plan includes a daily devotional and a daily "Bible Reading Plan."

The devotional will encourage and strengthen you as you set aside time to seek God during this season. The topics of the daily devotions are focused on cultivating your spiritual hunger through prayer, fasting, and drawing near to God.

Just like prayer and fasting, reading your Bible is about connecting to God in a more powerful way. It is not about duty but about relationship. When we engage God through reading His Word, we engage the very presence of God. His Word is living and active! As we read our Bible, we are drawing closer to God and positioning ourselves to hear from Him in particular ways.

Once again, as with prayer, choose the time and the place where you are going to read your Bible and devotional every single day, and come prepared to hear what He wants to tell you.

There are three quick things I'd like to share with you about how to get the most out of your devotional time with God.

1. Read Daily

It is better to read a little every day than to try and knock out two hours of Bible reading or devotions in one sitting. It is so important to digest the Word in absorbable chunks. The "Bible Reading Plan" I've included helps with that, as it leads you through about a chapter a day. Don't bite off more than you can chew, and certainly don't compare your "performance" with that of others. If you miss a few days, pick up at the next reading, but stay with it and don't give up.

The key is to keep this simple and make it sustainable. I predict that prayer and Bible reading will become the favorite part of your day!

2. Read Prayerfully

Talk to God as you're reading. Don't rush through. If you come across something you don't understand, pause for a moment and ask God about it. Reading prayerfully is making space and time to talk to God and giving Him time and space to talk to you. Taking time to meditate on God's Word is just as important as reading it.

3. Read with Expectation

You are about to partake of the bread of life, so foster an attitude of expectancy. Believe that God is going to speak to you through His Word. With meditation on the ideas and thoughts recorded in your journal, be prepared to do something with what He shows you.

A great, simple way to journal your devotionals is to use the SOAP method. (Wayne Cordeiro has some great material about this that I highly recommend in his book *Divine Mentor*.) SOAP stands for:

Scripture

Observation

Application

Prayer

The SOAP method works like this:

- *S for Scripture.* Read prayerfully. Take notice of which scripture(s) catches your attention and mark it in your Bible. When you're done, reread the verse(s) you marked and look for one that particularly speaks to you. Write it in your journal.

- *O for Observation.* Focusing on that scripture, tune in and listen to what God is saying to you through His Word. What is it about this scripture that specifically stands out? What does God want to reveal to you or teach you? Ask the Holy Spirit to be your guide and show you what God is saying.

- *A for Application.* Think of how this verse(s) applies to your life right now. Perhaps it is instruction, encouragement, revelation of a new promise, or correction for a particular area of your life. Use your journal to write how this scripture applies to you today.

- *P for Prayer.* Wrap up your SOAP time in prayer. Talk to God about what you've just read. This can be as simple as thanking Him for revealing a truth from the scripture, or it may be asking Him for greater insight or wisdom as to how it applies to your life. Remember, prayer is all about relationship. It's a two-way conversation, so be sure to listen to what God has to say.

That's it! SOAP. It's as simple or deep as you want it to be. If you want to go deeper in your study, here are additional tips:

- Reread the daily passage in a different Bible translation or paraphrase.

- Utilize online resources, such as those available from www. crosswalk.com.

- Utilize a commentary, such as those by Matthew Henry or online at www.biblegateway.com.

- Cross-reference your daily reading, using the footnotes in your study Bible.

- Research words in their original language using a *Strong's Concordance.*

My prayer for you over the next twenty-one days is that your passion for God and His Word will be ignited, and that you will develop a hunger for His presence that is greater than ever before!

FASTING

Important Note: Fasting requires reasonable precautions. If you have any health concerns, please consult your physician prior to beginning your fast, especially if you are taking medication, have a chronic condition, or are pregnant or nursing a baby.

As you prepare to fast, it is important to choose a fasting plan that works for you. While this section provides some general information about different types of fasts, as well as some suggestions on how to create your own fasting plan, I want to make clear that there's nothing more inherently spiritual about one type of fast as opposed to another. These are simply guidelines and suggestions on different things you can do.

Do not let what you eat or do not eat become the focus of your fast. Keep the main thing the main thing, which is drawing closer to God. Remember, this is a time to disconnect enough from your regular patterns and habits in order to connect more closely to God. Here are a few tips to keep in mind before getting started:

1. Start Where You Are

We are all at different places in our walk with God. Likewise our jobs, daily schedules, and health conditions are all different and place various levels of demand on our energy. So most importantly, whether you've fasted before or this is your first time, start where you are.

Your personal fast should present a level of challenge to it, but it's very important to know your own body, know your options and, most importantly, seek God in prayer and follow what the Holy Spirit leads you to do.

Remember, the goal of fasting is not just to do without food. The goal is to draw nearer to God.

2. Find Your Fast Zone

When I started fasting there was some discomfort, but I got used to the fasting routine pretty quickly. Quite simply, I learned how to fast in a way that worked for me.

I drank smoothies, juices, and even some coffee. As I progressed in fasting, I did different fasts in different seasons. I have done everything from long fasts (drinking only water) to fasting for a day (eating fruits and vegetables).

While any true fast does involve abstinence from food or at least certain types of food, I have found that different fasting combinations work better for different people. The goal to having a successful fast is all about finding what I call your Fast Zone, and that is different for everybody and can change depending on the season you are in.

The best way I can describe your Fast Zone is that it's the place where you feel light and spiritually in tune. Your mind is easily focused on God and spiritual things. You have an increased spiritual energy—you can feel the fast working. Just like runners know what their target heart rate is to see the benefits of their physical training, the Fast Zone is similar in a spiritual sense.

Finding your Fast Zone helps you choose both the type and length of fast. Let's say you choose to go on a Daniel fast (only fruits and vegetables). Should you eat beans? I don't know, but I will say that if you can eat beans and stay in *your* Fast Zone, go ahead. But for some people eating beans takes them out of the zone. Should you eat peanut butter? Probably not. Peanut butter is more of an indulgence, and I have never met a person who could stay in a Fast Zone while enjoying indulgences.

> The goal to having a successful fast is all about finding what I call your Fast Zone.

Should you completely cut out caffeine? It depends. The great thing is, when you fast, your body automatically craves less caffeine. If you can stay in your Fast Zone with a little caffeine, great. If you are going on a longer fast and want to cut it out of your diet completely, that's great too. But ease yourself off and make it your goal to be completely caffeine free about two-thirds of the way into your fast.

I will say that if you drink coffee regularly, one of the worst mistakes you can make is to fast for one to three days and cut caffeine out abruptly and completely. Please don't do that or you will spend this time grumpy and in withdrawal instead of enjoying God's presence. Chill out—coffee is bean juice. Have a cappuccino and draw close to Jesus!

I've also noticed that mixing things up a bit during a twenty-one-day fast works best for people. For example, do a fruits and vegetables fast for a week. Then do all liquids for a while. Maybe even mix in a few days of only water if you think you are ready for that. Then go back to fruits and vegetables for a few days. My point remains—find your Fast Zone!

Some people can't stay in a Fast Zone eating any type of solid food, so they prefer all liquids. With today's protein drinks and juicing machines, it is so easy to get a healthy dose of all your nutritional needs even while taking in only liquids. Certain people can't do anything other than drink only water. If they eat a salad or drink a glass of juice, they get out of their zone. Or if they allow themselves to eat cantaloupe, they will end up eating twenty cantaloupes a day!

I'll say it again: there isn't one approach that works the same for everyone. Some of my great fasts have been with only fruits and vegetables. Some other great fasts were water only. During my last extended fast, which was probably my best ever, I drank only fresh juices and whey protein drinks. Also, I always drink coffee during my fast. I just drink a lot less than I normally do. It's always different. Follow the Holy Spirit, mix it up, find what works for you, and stay in your Fast Zone!

3. Choose Your Type of Fast

While preparing for your fast, it is important to choose ahead of time what type of fast, or what combination, you will pursue. Not only will this help with making the necessary preparations to implement your plan, but as you commit to a specific fast ahead of time and know how you're going to do it, you will position yourself to finish strong.

On the following pages I list some options and variations of fasts you can choose from. As you read over the information, please consider how it may or may not apply to your personal circumstances and convictions.

You may choose to fast all twenty-one days. Or you may choose to fast several days out of the twenty-one days, such as three or four days a week throughout the twenty-one-day period. Maybe you will do that and do three to seven consecutive days at the end. This is your personal decision and should be prayerfully considered as it applies to your circumstances.

Specific Food or Activity Fast

In this type of fast you omit a specific item(s) from your meal plans. For example, you may choose to eliminate all red meat, processed or fast food, or sweets. Most people can incorporate this type of fast relatively easily. It can also prove to be a great solution for people with specific dietary needs or medical conditions that may cause certain limitations.

While fasting typically refers to refraining from specific food items, you may also find it extremely beneficial to fast from a regular activity or habit. This might include things such as television, social media, and the like. In fact, during your twenty-one days of dedicated prayer and fasting, I highly recommend fasting from television and things like news/talk radio as much as possible. This alone can change your life.

Remember, prayer and fasting are not just about connecting to God but also about disconnecting from the world. Tune out the other worldly voices as much as possible. Replace that time with reading God's Word and good Christian books. If you watch television, try to watch Christian programming or nature shows. Let your mind refresh.

Daniel Fast

The Daniel fast is a great model to follow and one that is extremely effective for spiritual focus, bodily discipline, and purification of the body and soul. It is probably one of the most commonly referred-to fasts; however, within the Daniel fast there is room for broad interpretation.

In the book of Daniel we find two different times where the prophet Daniel fasted. Daniel 1 states that he only ate vegetables and water, and in Daniel 10, while the passage does not give a specific list of foods that Daniel ate, it does state that he ate no rich (or choice) foods, as well as no meat or wine. So based on these two verses, we can see that either of these, or combinations of the two, constitute a Daniel fast.

Again, it is important to mention that there is nothing inherently spiritual about one type of fast as opposed to another. The foundation of the Daniel fast is fruits and vegetables. Some starchy vegetables and dairy could be included, but that depends on the individual. Your goal should be to seek God in prayer about this and follow what the Holy Spirit leads you to do. Just remember: find your personal Fast Zone.

Juice Fast

A juice fast is simply consuming vegetable and fruit juices and water instead of solid food. Many people include whey protein in their liquid plan as well. This is one of the most popular and effective fasts. Even if you choose not to make your entire fast liquids-only, substituting liquids for one or two meals is a great alternative.

Water Fast

A water-only fast is the normal fast referred to in the Bible. This is how Jesus and the New Testament church fasted. A water fast is just that—no eating of any food or drinking of any liquids except water.

I water fasted a lot more often when I was younger, but now I find I can't concentrate very well when I do. I only water fast when I know I can really get away and be by myself for a few days, and I would recommend the same thing to you. When Jesus went on His forty-day fast, He went by Himself out into the wilderness.

I've noticed with a water fast that I usually experience God more after the fast has ended. Yet when drinking only juices or eating vegetables I tend to experience God more during the fast. Both work well, but for some people it is hard to perform effectively at their jobs and have energy for their families while drinking only water.

I do recommend periodic water fasts, but extreme precautions should be taken. I would recommend consulting your physician first, and water fasting only for a day or two unless you can get away or your job allows you to really disconnect so you can give your best energy to the fast. You will experience some discomfort the first week or so but it will be worth it.

Having said all that, I know people who can water fast and work, and they function fine without much fatigue and are able to work well. You are blessed if you are one of these people.

Total Fast

A total fast is where nothing—neither liquid, solid food, nor even water—is consumed for a very short period of time. There are examples of this type of fast in the Bible. It was an Old Covenant type of fast associated with mourning or deep grief, such as when David engaged in a total fast for a week, hoping that God would spare the child he had with Bathsheba (2 Samuel 12).

Under the New Covenant, we do not fast to mourn or to seek forgiveness. God has already forgiven us, and we are commanded to celebrate Jesus because He is alive. Plus, complete abstinence of food and water can be very dangerous to our health. Attempting to go without water for any period of time can be extremely harmful to the body. *I strongly discourage the total fast.*

4. Begin and Break the Fast Well

Depending on the type of fast you choose, it is very important to prepare your body ahead of time before beginning the fast. Take a week or so to transition into your fast; otherwise, you could get sick. For example, if you would like to go on a fruits and vegetables or juice fast, start eliminating meat, white grains, and refined sugars from your diet the week before. Also start to cut back quite a bit on dairy products and some of your caffeine intake.

The same principle applies to breaking your fast. When your fast is over, add foods back in very gradually. Please don't break your fast with a greasy cheeseburger! Because your body is so cleansed and detoxified, you will most likely get sick if you do that.

There are also several supplements you can take that will help support the detox process during your fast. Your health-food store can give you recommendations.

FASTING WHILE NURSING OR PREGNANT

Strict fasting while pregnant or nursing also is not recommended. If you are in this incredible season of life but would like to participate in the twenty-one-day plan, here are some great options for you to consider—*with the approval of your physician:*

- a modified Daniel fast including whole grains, legumes, whey protein, calcium, and iron supplements
- fasting sweets and desserts
- fasting red meat
- fasting certain diversions (television shows, movies, social media—such as Facebook/Twitter, video games, and so on)

If you are a pregnant or nursing mother, your priority is the health and the development of the baby God has entrusted you with. Make that your guideline and go from there. And please consult your doctor.

FASTING AND EATING DISORDERS

If you have struggled with an eating disorder, this situation is a battle of the mind you *can win* through Christ (Philippians 4:13). Remember, fasting is a tool used to get closer to God, and it actually should keep us from being preoccupied with food. If your method of fasting is going to cause you to obsess about what you eat in any way, you will need to change either your approach or your mind-set.

If giving up food is a stumbling block to you, then consider fasting of television, reading (other than the Bible, of course), social media, or shopping. There are many distractions and ways that we use to stay in control that we could eliminate from our daily routine. We do these things to distract ourselves from the real issues hurting us. If you can identify such other things, maybe you can give those up instead of food.

The main thing I encourage you to do is remember that you are covered by God's grace. God will show you what to do. His "yoke is easy" and His "burden is light" (Matthew 11:30). His way will bring rest to your soul.

SAMPLE MENUS

I will share a few simple menu options for your use in the twenty-one-day fast. Your plan could include one of these menu ideas or even a variation of all of them. You could even mix it up, doing something different foodwise on the weekends or on certain days of the week. Again, pray about this and find what works for you.

To keep your energy up throughout the day, it's important to eat or drink every two and a half to three hours. If you go longer than that, you can experience an energy lull and be tempted to overstuff yourself at your next meal. Even if you're fasting on fruits and vegetables, overstuffing is never a smart thing to do.

It is very important to drink lots of water while fasting. I recommend about one hundred ounces of water per day to support your critical liver function. The liver is the filter for the body, so when you don't drink enough water, the liver doesn't function at its highest capacity.

Select your food items wisely. I'm not going to get into specific ingredients you should or should not include in your plan. The key is to prepare a plan ahead of the fast, to not get legalistic about it, and to choose menu items well. For example, if you prefer dressing on your salads, choose a healthy, organic option with natural ingredients—and don't pour a gallon of it on your plate.

If you're drinking fruit juices, try to go as natural as possible, and don't drink ones heavily processed and laden with sugar. Remember to not let food become the focus of your fast, but make wise eating choices.

Sample Menu 1: Fruits, Vegetables, Juices, and Water

Breakfast
Fruit smoothie with whey protein

Mid-morning Snack
Fresh fruit or fresh vegetables

Lunch
Raw vegetable salad with light, organic dressing and vegetable broth soup

Mid-afternoon Snack
Fresh fruit or fresh vegetables

Dinner
Fresh salad with light, organic dressing and steamed or grilled vegetables

Water
Drink plenty of water—at least 100 ounces—throughout the day to assist with the detoxifying process.

Sample Menu 2: Liquids Only

Breakfast
Fruit smoothie with whey protein

Mid-morning Snack
Herbal tea or vegetable broth soup

Lunch

Raw, juiced vegetables

Mid-afternoon Snack

Fresh fruit juice or fruit smoothie with whey protein

Dinner

Vegetable juice or vegetable broth soup

Water

Drink plenty of water—at least 100 ounces—throughout the day to assist with the detoxifying process.

Sample Menu 3: Modified Daniel Fast

Breakfast

1–2 servings whole grains with fresh fruit juice

Mid-morning Snack

Fresh fruit or fresh chopped vegetables

Lunch

1–2 servings whole grains; fresh salad with legumes and light, organic dressing

Mid-afternoon Snack

Fresh fruit juice or fruit smoothie with whey protein

Dinner

1–2 whole grains; fresh salad with legumes and light, organic dressing

Water

Drink plenty of water—at least 100 ounces—throughout the day to assist with the detoxifying process.

FINAL TIPS

Here are some other ideas that can help make your fasting experience more pleasant and helpful:

- As you select your type of fast, make a fasting calendar that fits your plan. Determine what each day and week will look like. (See pages 144–45 for an example.)

- Keep your fridge and pantry stocked with the items you need. Being unprepared to fast sets you up to give into temptation. Choose well when selecting products, stick to raw food as much as you can, limit artificial ingredients, and keep tempting foods out of the kitchen.

- Make it a priority to attend church during your twenty-one-day fast. Being around other believers will encourage you to keep on going when fasting gets difficult.

- If you are fasting with others, you may want to do a weekly small group. Use the "Small Group Study Guide" (found on page 199) to help facilitate this.

- If you mess up, don't get discouraged. Just get right back on track and keep going. God's mercies "are new every morning" (Lamentations 3:22–23). He wants you to finish, and He will give you the grace and strength to do it.

God be with you as you begin your awakening adventure!

FASTING

Plan your fasting week	SUNDAY	MONDAY	TUESDAY
	Day 1	Day 2	Day 3
	Day 8	Day 9	Day 10
	Day 15	Day 16	Day 17

My Personal Fasting Plan: (List here what foods or activities you will be fasting.)

_____

_____

_____

_____

_____

CALENDAR

WEDNESDAY	THURSDAY	FRIDAY	SATURDAY
Day 4	Day 5	Day 6	Day 7
Day 11	Day 12	Day 13	Day 14
Day 18	Day 19	Day 20	Day 21

During this fast, I am praying and believing God for:

_____

_____

_____

_____

_____

_____

Return to Me

> "Even now," declares the LORD, "return to me with all
> your heart, with fasting and weeping and mourning."
>
> JOEL 2:12, NIV

I F WE LOOK AT THE KIND OF FASTING that took place in the Old Testament, it would be easy to assume that the reason we fast is to prove our repentance to God in order to obtain His mercy. Under the Old Covenant, such a fast of repentance is seen time and again. But now, because of the complete work of Jesus on the cross, things have changed.

Fasting is not something we do to obtain favor or forgiveness. Under the New Covenant, every wrong we have done and will do was forgiven at the Cross, and when we accept Christ as our Savior, we get to celebrate the mercy freely given to us through our relationship with Him. Fasting is about drawing closer to God and surrendering at a deeper level.

As we walk with God, there are times that we feel far from Him or disconnected. Joel's words resonate with us, even if we live in a context of grace: "Return to me with all your heart." There are times we realize that though we have chosen to follow Jesus, the flame of our love for Him has grown cold.

Your time spent in prayer each day of the

> We don't have to fast for forgiveness.
> Every wrong we have done and will
> do was forgiven at the Cross.

fast can result in a new richness, a rewarding connection with the Father. No matter where you are on your journey with Jesus, you can always take a step closer toward Him.

> *I believe the power of fasting as it relates to prayer is the spiritual atomic bomb that our Lord has given us to destroy the strongholds of evil and usher in a great revival and spiritual harvest around the world.* —BILL BRIGHT

Bible Reading Plan: Psalms 1–2

Prayer Focus: As we begin this time of prayer and fasting, let's turn our hearts toward God. Make a commitment to seek Him daily. Pray that your love for Christ will be increased and your passion for Him will be reignited over the next twenty-one days.

Optional Book Reading Plan: Chapter 1, pages 1–4 (stop at "Live on a Mountaintop?")

The Awakening Journey

_____

_____

_____

_____

_____

_____

_____

_____

_____

_____

Tune In

My sheep hear My voice, and I know them, and
they follow Me.

—JOHN 10:27

HAVE YOU EVER TRIED TO TUNE IN a radio station only to be
frustrated by finding static rather than music? And when you fid-
dled with the dial again, suddenly you heard a clear signal. The fact is that
clear signal always existed on the airwaves. The difference is that now you
have adjusted your tuner to the right frequency.

In our hectic lives, there are so many signals bombarding our senses that
it can become difficult to distinguish God's voice from the deafening static
noise of life. Fasting enables us to tune out the world's distractions and *tune
in* to God. As we fast, we deny our flesh. When we deny our flesh, we become
more in tune to the Holy Spirit
and can hear God's voice more
clearly. If you truly listen for
God's voice, you will hear it.
And when you hear it, your faith
will increase.

> Fasting enables us to tune
> out the world's distractions
> and *tune in* to God.

If you desire to tune out the static of life and really tune in to the voice of
God, come to Him first and foremost with ears willing to listen and a heart
ready to obey what He says (Psalm 34:18; Isaiah 66:2). The more we practice
being in His presence, the clearer and more recognizable His voice becomes.

Fasting is important, more important, perhaps, than many of us have supposed.... When exercised with a pure heart and a right motive, fasting may provide us with a key to unlock doors where others may have failed; a window opening up new horizons in the unseen world; a spiritual weapon of God's providing, "mighty to the pulling down of strongholds." —ARTHUR WALLIS

Bible Reading: Luke 1

Prayer Focus: In this time of fasting, what is your mind tuned to? What distractions do you need to remove so that you can focus on God? Prepare your heart to hear the voice of God, and ask Him to help you remove distractions that keep you from focusing on Him and hearing His voice clearly.

Optional Book Reading Plan: Chapter 1, beginning at page 4 ("Live on a Mountaintop?") through end of chapter

The Awakening Journey

_____

_____

_____

_____

_____

_____

_____

_____

_____

_____

_____

DAY 3

Fasting Removes Unbelief

Jesus rebuked the demon, and it came out of him; and the child was cured from that very hour. Then the disciples came to Jesus privately and said, "Why could we not cast it out?" So Jesus said to them, "Because of your unbelief; for assuredly, I say to you, if you have faith as a mustard seed, you will say to this mountain, 'Move from here to there,' and it will move; and nothing will be impossible for you. However, this kind does not go out except by prayer and fasting."

—MATTHEW 17:18–21

WHEN WE PRAY AND FAST, we don't do so to change God or His will; instead, by praying and fasting, we are the ones changed. Coming into alignment with God helps us curb our doubts and fears. When we pray and fast, the thing that leaves—the thing that goes out—is our unbelief. It is when we have faith to believe that we can pray with confidence and know that "nothing will be impossible."

Ask God to strengthen your heart to fully believe Him and His Word. It is okay to recognize and acknowledge if you struggle with unbelief. That's the first step in allowing God to strengthen your faith and bring you into alignment with His plan for your life.

> When we pray and fast, we don't do so to change God or His will; by praying and fasting, we are the ones changed.

Beware in your prayers, above everything else, of limiting
God, not only by unbelief, but by fancying that you know
what He can do. Expect..."above all that we ask or think."
—ANDREW MURRAY

Bible Reading Plan: Luke 2

Prayer Focus: What do you need faith to believe for? Align yourself with God's Word and will during this fast. Release your unbelief. Pray with confidence, knowing "nothing will be impossible" for you.

Optional Book Reading Plan: Chapter 2

The Awakening Journey

_____

_____

_____

_____

_____

_____

_____

FASTING TIP

On the third day of your fast, you may experience a headache, flu-like achiness, intense sugar or carb cravings, slight nausea, or fatigue. This is a normal response to detoxification, so make sure you allow yourself some time to rest and keep your fluid intake high. The fourth day is usually much better physically, so hang in there!

Agreement with the Will of God

Can two walk together, unless they are agreed?
—AMOS 3:3

I N THE HEART OF EVERY BELIEVER is the desire to walk closely with God. We know that He, too, desires a close relationship with each one of us. A key to having a strong level of spiritual intimacy with God is living in agreement with His will for your life.

In Genesis 5:22, we read of Enoch and see that his life modeled a long journey, walking consistently with God, for it says, "Enoch walked with God three hundred years." Enoch lived a powerful life. He was a man who walked in agreement with God's will and lived a life pleasing to God (Hebrews 11:5).

It is one thing to *know* God's will for our lives; it's another to live in agreement

> The level of our agreement with God will determine the degree of closeness in our walk with Him.

with His will. In order to enjoy the best life that God has for us, we must first understand that God does not change, but we sometimes must. Let's earnestly seek to know and agree with God's will. The level of our agreement with God will determine the degree of closeness in our walk with Him.

I believe firmly, that the moment our hearts are emptied of pride and selfishness and ambition and self seeking, and everything that is contrary to God's law, the Holy Ghost will come and fill every corner of our hearts; but if we are full of pride and conceit, and ambition and self seeking, and pleasure and the world, there is no room for the Spirit of God; and I believe many a man is praying to God to fill him when he is full already with something else. Before we pray that God would fill us, I believe we ought to pray Him to empty us. —D. L. MOODY

Bible Reading Plan: Luke 3

Prayer Focus: Pray today that you can walk in agreement with God and enjoy the life He desires you to have in Christ.

Optional Book Reading Plan: Chapter 3, pages 15–18 (stop at "Passion Expresses Emotion")

The Awakening Journey

_____

_____

_____

_____

_____

_____

_____

_____

_____

_____

_____

When Grace Comes Down

For the law was given through Moses, but grace
and truth came through Jesus Christ.

—JOHN 1:17

HAVE YOU EVER WONDERED what it would be like to have a personal visit with God? What would He say about the state of humanity? about religion? about our propensity toward sin?

There is no need to wonder about what God is like or would say, because to know Him, we have only to look at Jesus. In Jesus we have received grace, but there is even something more we have received: *truth*.

The kind of truth in today's scripture is not a list of laws and rules such as were given to Moses. Make no mistake—the revelation of God through the word of the Law was glorious. When Moses came down from Mount Sinai after receiving the Ten Commandments, his face shone so brightly with the glory of God that he had to wear a veil (Exodus 34:33–35). But the word of the Law cannot compare with the word of *life* that has been revealed through Jesus Christ!

In John 1:18 we learn that no one, not even Moses, with his glimpse of God's back, has ever

> It is from a state of grace, not legalism, that we will find real and lasting transformation.

seen God. But Jesus has not only seen God—He *is* God. The truth that John was speaking about is a clear and unveiled vision of the true nature of God.

Looking at God through the lens of legalism and religion is like looking at Him through a veil. Only when we see Him though Jesus Christ can we truly get a glimpse into His heart. It is from a state of grace, not legalism, that we will find real and lasting transformation (2 Corinthians 3:7–18).

I am not what I ought to be, I am not what I want to be, I am not what I hope to be in another world; but still I am not what I once used to be, and by the grace of God I am what I am. —JOHN NEWTON

Bible Reading Plan: Luke 4

Prayer Focus: Have you been looking at God through the veil of legalism and religion? In Jesus, we see the full revelation of the nature of God: His love and holiness, mercy and justice, compassion and power all perfectly and beautifully expressed. Pray that the Holy Spirit will help you see God through the eyes of grace and truth given to us in Jesus Christ.

Optional Book Reading Plan: Chapter 3, beginning at page 18 ("Passion Expresses Emotion") through end of chapter

The Awakening Journey

_____

_____

_____

_____

_____

_____

_____

_____

The Spirit Is Willing

> And I know that nothing good lives in me, that is,
> in my sinful nature. I want to do what is right, but
> I can't. I want to do what is good, but I don't. I don't
> want to do what is wrong, but I do it anyway. But if
> I do what I don't want to do, I am not really the one
> doing wrong; it is sin living in me that does it.
>
> —ROMANS 7:18–20, NLT

THERE'S AN INTERNAL WAR THAT RAGES within each of us. Paul described this so well in Romans 7. Though we desire to do the right thing, we don't have the power to do so in our own efforts and we mess up.

The good news is that we don't have to rely on our own strength to make right decisions. We don't have to be dominated by our sinful nature and end up doing the things we don't want to do. But the only way we can live this kind of life is by yielding to the Holy Spirit and relying on the strength of Jesus Christ, not our own.

> When we're facing struggles, we must rely on God's power alive within us through the Holy Spirit.

When we're facing struggles, we must rely on God's power alive within us through the Holy Spirit. When we are born again, the Holy Spirit resides in us and places in us the desire to do what is pleasing to God (Hebrews

10:16). The Holy Spirit always wants to do what is right and to uphold the perfect will of God, pleasing the Father in every way.

It is our job to lay down our stubborn fleshly will and yield to the will of God. In that moment, the Holy Spirit will be there to help us. Let's learn to yield to and become totally reliant upon the Holy Spirit.

> *[Prayer] turns ordinary mortals into men of power. It brings power. It brings fire. It brings rain. It brings life. It brings God.* —SAMUEL CHADWICK

Bible Reading Plan: Proverbs 1

Prayer Focus: Are there areas in your life causing an internal struggle? Make a decision today to yield to the Holy Spirit and lean on His strength, not your own, to overcome obstacles of sin and selfishness in your life. Surrender and release those areas to God, knowing He will help you.

Optional Book Reading Plan: Chapter 4, pages 23–28 (stop at "The Trap of Performance")

The Awakening Journey

_____

_____

_____

_____

_____

_____

_____

_____

_____

_____

Fervent Prayer

> The effective, fervent prayer of a righteous man
> avails much.
>
> —JAMES 5:16

FERVENCY SPEAKS TO OUR LEVEL of intensity, passion, and persistence. Many times, we can lose our passion in prayer or stop praying for certain things altogether because we lose heart or give up. But God invites us to keep them before Him and trust Him for an answer in His time (Matthew 7:7–11).

The Old Testament prophet Elijah practiced a lifestyle of fervent, intense prayer and witnessed incredible miracles in his lifetime. In the book of Kings, the story is told of a woman whose only son became ill and died (1 Kings 17:17–24). When Elijah heard the news, he quickly took action and did what he knew best—he fervently cried out to God. Elijah fully believed that God could bring the boy back to life, and he prayed not just once but three times that the boy's soul would return to him. He prayed fervently and repeatedly and he wasn't going to give up. This

> Many times, we can lose our passion in prayer or stop praying for certain things altogether because we lose heart or give up. But God invites us to keep them before Him and trust Him for an answer in His time.

was the result: "Then the LORD heard the voice of Elijah; and the soul of the child came back to him, and he revived" (verse 22).

Elijah's prayer was answered through his persistence and fervency. God hears your prayers as well and will bring an answer in His perfect timing. But don't be discouraged or disheartened if the answer takes time to arrive or is not exactly what you expected. Commit to praying to God with passion and persistence, trusting the answer will come in God's perfect way at the perfect time.

> *We must never forget that the highest kind of prayer is never the making of requests. Prayer at its holiest moment is the entering into God to a place of such blessed union as makes miracles seem tame and remarkable answers to prayer appear something very far short of wonderful by comparison.* —A. W. TOZER

Bible Reading Plan: Psalms 3–5

Prayer Focus: As you close out this first week, continue to pray fervently for the main areas of concern in your life. Trust God to bring an answer as you journal your thoughts and inspirations through this time.

Optional Book Reading Plan: Chapter 4, beginning at page 28 ("The Trap of Performance") through end of chapter

The Awakening Journey

_____

_____

_____

_____

_____

Week Two of Your Fast

ENTERING WEEK TWO OF YOUR FAST can present a different level of challenge. Although you probably experienced a decrease in cravings after day three, you may now be experiencing a resurgence of those same cravings.

Right around this time, a metabolic shift takes place in your body. If you are consuming significantly fewer calories than you were before, your body naturally shifts to its own resources to find sufficient fuel. These hunger pangs you are feeling right now are basically your body asking, "Hey, what's up? Are you going to give me some more calories, or should I move on to the next available source?" That next source means reserves stored mostly in your fat cells and somewhat in your muscles.

During the second week it is so important to remind yourself *why* you are doing this. This is when we truly realize how weak we really are, how much we need God's strength and grace, and not only physically to keep us from eating. We need His grace to be more compassionate, slow to anger, less judgmental, more pliable, more forgiving, and more generous.

Over the next couple of days, if you stick to your fast, here's what will happen to your body:

1. Your metabolism will slow down. In other words, it will shift to a mode of operation where it requires less energy—or calories— to function.

2. A cycle of internal consumption will begin to use your energy stores in the form of fat—and some muscle. To minimize muscle breakdown, drink two glasses of whey protein a day.
3. Because toxins that we consume and don't eliminate are stored mostly in fat, you will also hit a new level of detox as your body starts using up your fat reserves.

Hang in there! The best is yet to come.

Hear Him

> "This is my dearly loved Son, who brings me great
> joy. Listen to him."… And when they looked up,
> Moses and Elijah were gone, and they saw only Jesus.
> —MATTHEW 17:5, 8, NLT

O N THE MOUNT OF TRANSFIGURATION three disciples had an experience that showed us the Father's plan for the New Covenant. Jesus took Peter, James, and John up to the top of a mountain where He was transfigured into His glorified state. Up until this point, the Jews had related to God through the Law—represented by Moses and the prophets, one being Elijah. Inspired by what he was seeing, Peter eagerly offered to erect three tabernacles—one each for Jesus, Moses, and Elijah. Then a loud voice from heaven was heard: "This is my dearly loved Son, who brings me great joy. Listen to him."

When the disciples looked up, they saw only Jesus.

On that mountain God made it clear that

> You cannot earn God's pleasure, but you can experience it to a greater degree as you follow Jesus Christ.

we will only discover His pleasure by following Jesus. God's grace is freely given to those who receive new life in Him. Sometimes, though, there are areas of our lives where we do not fully embrace God's grace. There may be circumstances or areas where we still try to earn our way to the Father.

You cannot earn God's pleasure, but you can experience it to a greater degree as you follow Jesus Christ. As you seek God today, ask Him for a greater revelation of Jesus in your heart. Then will you be reminded that you are a beloved child of God. And that He finds *pleasure* in you.

> *If heaven were by merit, it would never be heaven to me, for if I were in it I should say, "I am sure I am here by mistake; I am sure this is not my place; I have no claim to it." But if it be of grace and not of works, then we may walk into heaven with boldness.* —CHARLES H. SPURGEON

Bible Reading Plan: Luke 5

Prayer Focus: How does understanding the New Covenant of grace change the focus of your fast? As you pray and seek after God, let His be the loudest voice you hear.

Optional Book Reading Plan: Chapter 5, pages 37–41 (stop at "When You Fast")

The Awakening Journey

FASTING TIP

On day eight you might experience:

- fatigue—let yourself have extra rest if you need it
- achiness and a headache
- irritability
- fogginess

All of these symptoms are normal and will pass. Make sure you keep your water intake up. If you're eating fruits and vegetables that contain a lot of water, you may not have a desire to drink much water. However, keeping your water intake up will help you flush out the second round of toxins that your body is releasing and help relieve the symptoms more quickly.

Finally, more than ever this is the time you have to be vigilant about your spiritual focus. Great days are ahead, and you will be so glad you pushed through this day and didn't give up!

Clean House

> For those who live according to the flesh set their minds on
> the things of the flesh, but those who live according to the
> Spirit, the things of the Spirit. For to be carnally minded is
> death, but to be spiritually minded is life and peace.
> —ROMANS 8:5–6

HAVE YOU EVER LOOKED AT THE top of your refrigerator or in the deep recesses of your couch cushions and noticed the filth that has built up over time? Even though we might clean on a regular basis, there are times when we need to go...a little deeper. We realize that what appeared to be clean on the surface was in all actuality, quite filthy.

The same thing can happen spiritually. As we go about our daily lives, there are things that can build up over time. Even if we worship, pray, and read our Bible regularly, the different temptations, pressures, and cares of this world can build up quietly and end up consuming our lives. Without even realizing it, we can lose our peace, joy, and passion for the things of God. Our service to God, which used to fill us with life and excitement, becomes a tiresome duty that we must fulfill.

Fasting is the deep cleaning that

> Fasting is the deep cleaning that helps us take our mind off the things of this world and instead have a refreshed focus on the things of the Spirit.

helps us take our minds off the things of this world and instead have a refreshed focus on the things of the Spirit. Fasting offers an incredibly effective way to get into the nooks and crannies of our souls and bring all those dusty old habits, broken mind-sets, and rusty attitudes out into the light of God's truth.

In fasting and prayer, our service to God returns to something we *want to* do rather than something we *have to* do.

> *One of the reasons for fasting is to know what is in us.... In fasting it will come out. You will see it. And you will have to deal with it quickly or smother it again.* —JOHN PIPER

Bible Reading Plan: Luke 6

Prayer Focus: As you pray and fast today, ask God to show you any areas where you could use a refreshed spiritual focus. Pray as David did in Psalm 51:10–12 that God will cleanse your heart, renew your spirit, and restore the joy of your salvation. Pray with confidence, knowing that He wants to fill you with His life and peace.

Optional Book Reading Plan: Chapter 5, beginning at page 41 ("When You Fast") through end of chapter

The Awakening Journey

_____

_____

_____

_____

_____

_____

Unwavering Faith

But let him ask in faith, nothing wavering.

—JAMES 1:6, KJV

WHAT DO YOU EXPECT WHEN YOU PRAY? When we pray with earnest expectation, we are exercising our faith. The earnest prayer of righteous people produces powerful results (James 5:16, NLT), and the most earnest prayers come from us when we recognize our need for God.

There can be a natural tendency to shrink back when praying for the seemingly impossible, but we must remember that nothing is impossible with God (Luke 1:37). If we know the promises that God has given us, and understand His character and the principles by which He works, we can pray with confidence and trust Him for the answer.

What has caused you to waver in your expectation with God? James reminds us that faith and wavering are actually contradictory—James says "nothing wavering." Know that God never wavers in His love for you. You can trust Him completely.

> The most earnest prayers come from us when we recognize our need for God.

There is no way that Christians in a private capacity can do so much to promote the work of God and advance the kingdom of Christ as by prayer.
—JONATHAN EDWARDS

When we depend upon organizations, we get what organizations can do; when we depend upon education, we get what education can do; when we depend upon man, we get what man can do; but when we depend upon prayer, we get what God can do. —A.C. DIXON

Bible Reading Plan: Luke 7

Prayer Focus: What are you trusting God for in this season? How can you line up your expectations with the Word of God when you pray? Find promises in His Word that answer your need and write them down today.

Optional Book Reading Plan: Chapter 11

The Awakening Journey

_____

_____

_____

_____

_____

_____

_____

_____

Prayer and the Process

Seven times Elijah told him to go and look. Finally the seventh time, his servant told him, "I saw a little cloud about the size of a man's hand rising from the sea." Then Elijah shouted, "Hurry to Ahab and tell him, 'Climb into your chariot and go back home. If you don't hurry, the rain will stop you!'"

—1 KINGS 18:43–44, NLT

H OW DO I KNOW GOD is going to say *yes* to my prayers?" This is a common question many people have as they seek a confident prayer life. However, it's important to recognize that prayer is not just about the answer; it's also about glorifying God in the process of waiting for the answer. It is our responsibility to check our motives and believe God hears us.

We see an example of the process of prayer in this story of Elijah (1 Kings 18). Elijah climbed to the top of the mountain to pray for rain to come. As he waited for the rain, he continued to pray, believing God would answer.

> Prayer is not just about the answer; it's also about glorifying God in the process of waiting for the answer.

When he finally saw a small cloud, he told Ahab to get ready because the rain was coming. Elijah knew what to pray for, and God heard him the first time he prayed. But there was preparation that needed to take place in order for Elijah to receive the answer to his prayer.

It is no mistake that God waited until Elijah had prayed seven times before He answered. In the Bible, seven represents completion. In this story, seven represents the completion of God's process regarding Elijah's prayer request.

God does not want merely to answer our prayers; He wants to spend time with us to prepare us for the answer that will come. Many times we want to skip over the process involved in engaging God in prayer as we wait for our answer. But it is this very process that works maturity in us and prepares us for the answers our prayers bring (James 1:4).

> *The reason why many fail in battle is because they wait until the hour of battle. The reason why others succeed is because they have gained their victory on their knees long before the battle came. Anticipate your battles; fight them on your knees before temptation comes, and you will always have victory.* —R. A. TORREY

Bible Reading Plan: Luke 8

Prayer Focus: What prayers of yours are still awaiting an answer? Throughout this fast, thank God for His process at work in you…and trust Him.

Optional Book Reading Plan: Chapter 6, pages 49–56 (stop at "Fervent Prayer")

The Awakening Journey

_____

_____

_____

_____

_____

_____

DAY 12 ☑

Praying Boldly

> And it came to pass, at the time of the offering of the
> evening sacrifice, that Elijah the prophet came near and said,
> "LORD God of Abraham, Isaac, and Israel, let it be known
> this day that You are God in Israel and I am Your servant."
> —1 KINGS 18:36

T HE SACRIFICE REFERENCED ABOVE was a declaration that Elijah
was a servant of the Most High God. Elijah belonged to God, and he
represented God to the people. However, Elijah's boldness was not a result of
who *he* was; it was the result of knowing *God*!

As children of God under the New Covenant, we don't have to be timid
or fearful when coming to God in prayer. We can approach Him boldly.

> Let us then fearlessly and confidently and boldly draw near to the
> throne of grace (the throne of God's unmerited favor to us sinners),
> that we may receive mercy [for our failures] and find grace to help in
> good time for every need [appropriate help and well-timed help,
> coming just when we need it]. (Hebrews 4:16, AMP)

It's intimidating to think about taking a fearless, confident, bold attitude
when coming before God in prayer. Yet this is exactly what we are admonished to do! God has already settled the issue of our access to Him, but we
can be assured our access is not because of our own righteousness. It's because
of what Jesus did on the cross.

We can come to the throne in such outrageous boldness because Jesus was outrageously righteous! When we pray, we come to God in the authority of Jesus' name, and we can be confident that we will find grace, mercy, and perfectly timed help.

> *Fasting is not an end in itself; it is a means by which we can worship the Lord and submit ourselves in humility to Him. We don't make God love us any more than He already does if we fast, or if we fast longer.... [Fasting] invites God into the problem. Then in the strength of God, victory is possible.* —ELMER L. TOWNS

Bible Reading Plan: Luke 9

Prayer Focus: Do you approach God with timidity or confidence? Seek God boldly today knowing you are fully forgiven and Jesus has made you righteous. When you approach God in prayer, seek a fresh revelation of who He is in your life.

Optional Book Reading Plan: Chapter 6, beginning at page 56 ("Fervent Prayer") through end of chapter

The Awakening Journey

_____

_____

_____

_____

_____

_____

_____

Cultivating Spiritual Hunger

> Immediately the Spirit drove Him into the wilderness. And He
> was there in the wilderness forty days, tempted by Satan, and
> was with the wild beasts; and the angels ministered to Him.
>
> —MARK 1:12–13

EVEN JESUS DISCONNECTED FROM THE WORLD to fast and pray. Matthew, Mark, and Luke tell of Jesus going to the wilderness for forty days and forty nights. They also describe other times Jesus pulled away from the demands of the crowds, His ministry, and even His closest friends to pray.

There are times that we, too, need to pull away from the things of the world and focus on God. "The things of the world" can certainly include more than just food. In fact, in our world they are more likely television, movies, Facebook, Twitter, cell phones, and the Internet. None of these things are wrong in and of themselves, but they are avenues for a mental and spiritual crowd to gather around us and drown out the Holy Spirit's voice.

> Fasting is a means of disconnecting from the distractions of daily life and consciously choosing to bring God into greater focus.

Fasting is a means of disconnecting from the distractions of daily life and consciously choosing to bring God into greater focus. Giving up physical nourishment is the first step in engaging that process. If you think about it, though, in day-to-day life we nourish our souls as well as our bodies. We do so through reading, talking, socializing, playing, and entertainment. When our souls are full of those things, we often don't hunger for God.

During this time of fasting, we are sure to feel physical hunger, but let's be intentional about cultivating spiritual hunger as well. Let's draw away from the crowd and lay aside for a season the activities we use to nourish our souls. Instead let's enter a state of spiritual hunger, a craving for righteousness. Jesus said that being spiritually hungry is a blessed state, because there we can be sure of being filled with food that truly satisfies our deepest needs (Matthew 5:6).

Fasting helps to express, to deepen, and to confirm the resolution that we are ready to sacrifice anything, to sacrifice ourselves, to attain what we seek for the kingdom of God.... Prayer is the reaching out after God and the unseen; fasting the letting go of all that is of the seen and temporal. —ANDREW MURRAY

Bible Reading Plan: Psalms 6–7

Prayer Focus: During this time, you will find that being still before the Lord will set you in a place of increased strength, peace, and hunger for God. Are you disconnected from things that nourish your body and soul? What do you need to deny yourself to make this a powerful time in your life?

Optional Book Reading Plan: Chapter 7, pages 63–68 (stop at "Fasting Gets the Gunk Out")

The Awakening Journey

_____

_____

_____

_____

_____

Alignment with Heaven

Thy kingdom come, Thy will be done in
earth, as it is in heaven.
—MATTHEW 6:10, KJV

W E HAVE ALL HEARD THE PHRASE, "just like heaven on earth."
When Jesus taught His disciples how to pray in Matthew 6:9–13,
He provided some insight into what "heaven on earth" might look like.

In reality, heaven is a place where God's will reigns supreme. If we want
to have a taste of heaven on earth, then our prayer should be like Jesus': "Thy
kingdom come, Thy will be done…" The purest motivation for our prayers
is that God will be glorified and that His will would reign supreme in our
lives, just as it does in heaven.

On a more personal level,
we can pray that His will be
unhindered in our own life.
Rather than imposing His
will upon us, God gives us
the choice to surrender to it
with trust and gladness. As
we yield to the Lordship of
Christ over every area of our lives, we come into agreement with Him. We
experience alignment with heaven and position ourselves to taste a little bit of
heaven here on earth.

> The purest motivation for
> our prayers is that God will
> be glorified and that His will
> would reign supreme in our
> lives, just as it does in heaven.

God's will then becomes what we desire and the thing we most seek after. We enter into the incredible adventure of participating in God's plan to move His kingdom forward on the earth. This is where we find the most fulfilling and joyous life, but it all starts with one personal "yes, Lord" on our part.

> *All that God is, and all that God has, is at the disposal of prayer.... Prayer can do anything that God can do, and as God can do anything, prayer is omnipotent.*
> —R. A. TORREY

> *Our prayers lay the track down on which God's power can come. Like a mighty locomotive, his power is irresistible, but it cannot reach us without rails.* —WATCHMAN NEE

Bible Reading Plan: Luke 10

Prayer Focus: What does God's will "on earth as it is in heaven" look like in your life? Do the desires of your heart line up with the will of God? As we seek God together, let's pray as Jesus taught us, "Thy kingdom come, Thy will be done."

Optional Book Reading Plan: Chapter 7, beginning at page 68 ("Fasting Gets the Gunk Out") through end of chapter

The Awakening Journey

_____

_____

_____

_____

_____

Questions Along the Way

WhﾱAT IF I STUMBLE, WHAT IF I FALL?"

"What if I mess up and eat something not on my plan?"

"What if I just can't go without something—like caffeine—as I had planned to?"

"Will God still honor my fast?"

I remember the time a few years ago when someone asked me if I had ever "messed up" on a fast. I had to laugh because, of course, the answer was a huge yes. It has actually taken me years of developing a lifestyle of fasting to build up to where I am now. Over time, fasting does get easier, but this is a spiritual activity where it's easy for condemnation to try and take root. Don't let that happen!

Choosing to start a fast is quite similar to setting goals in life. It is good for us to challenge ourselves and set the bar high. Each time I prepare for a fast, I set goals that are typically beyond what I did the last time, and they're always beyond what I know I can do in my own strength. When we set the bar high, sometimes the natural result is failure to meet the goal. But that should never stop us from trying to reach as high as we can. So what if you mess up? What should you do then? Proverbs 24:16 says, "For though a righteous man falls seven times, he rises again, but the wicked are brought down by calamity" (NIV).

This "fall down, get back up" idea has been a formative principle in my life in so many areas, and it's no different in the arena of devotion to God. What matters is not that we stumble, but that we get back up! True failure only occurs when we let adversity keep us down.

Maybe you have tried to participate in this fast but have found yourself stumbling along the way. I want to encourage you to try it again during this last week. Don't be discouraged by looking at the times you gave in to hunger or messed up. But be encouraged by this: when we draw near to God, He draws near to us (James 4:8). He wants to draw near to you, so keep it up! I am confident that you will be rewarded and blessed for your perseverance.

The Spoken Word

> When he had said this, Jesus called in a loud
> voice, "Lazarus, come out!"
> —JOHN 11:43, NIV

THE STORY OF LAZARUS'S DEATH and resurrection reflects the power of Jesus' spoken word. Jesus was so in tune with the will of His Father that He already knew in His heart the miracle that was about to take place, but His words spoke the miracle into existence.

While prayer is our declaration of our dependence on God, our spoken words can be the manifestation of what's happening in our hearts. There is power in our spoken words, whether they are used to build up or tear down. It is important to keep our hearts filled with the truth from God's Word so that our words will produce good fruit.

As you seek God in prayer, ask Him for discernment to know a need and the words to help someone today.

> While prayer is our declaration of our dependence on God, our spoken words can be the manifestation of what's happening in our hearts.

Pray that your words would be encouraging, edifying, and aligned with the truth of God's Word. Building others up around us with our words allows us to be God's instrument to accomplish His good work.

*The key to praying with power is to become the kind of
persons who do not use God for our ends but are utterly
devoted to being used for his ends.* —JOHN PIPER

*I am persuaded that love and humility are the highest
attainments in the school of Christ, and the brightest
evidences that he is indeed our master.*
—JOHN NEWTON

Bible Reading Plan: Luke 11

Prayer Focus: As God continues to fill you through this season of prayer
and fasting, He wants to take what is now in your heart and share it with
others. How can you use the power of your spoken words to speak God's
truth in the lives of others?

Optional Book Reading Plan: Chapter 8, pages 73–75 (stop at
"Alignment")

The Awakening Journey

_____

_____

_____

_____

_____

_____

_____

_____

_____

FASTING TIP

For many, week three feels like a breakthrough week! By now your body should be thoroughly detoxified, and if you success-fully navigated that metabolic shift that happened in week two, you're likely to find yourself coasting until day twenty-one.

As your body has become used to less food, you are more than likely experiencing fewer hunger pangs. Since your body has detoxified, you are most likely also experiencing less achi-ness and headaches. Because your body is not using as much energy to digest food, it can devote more energy into the restor-ative processes. During this last week you may also find you are sleeping better too.

Spiritually speaking, this week can be really powerful as you find yourself in your Fast Zone and your mind has made the leap to focusing more on God.

Taking Off the Grave Clothes

Jesus said to them, "Take off the grave
clothes and let him go."

—JOHN 11:44, NIV

WHEN IT COMES TO THE TRANSFORMING power of God
working in someone's life, God often uses people to bring about
divine life change. The story of Lazarus in John 11 illustrates how it was the
power of Jesus' prayer and spoken word that resurrected Lazarus from the
dead, but the disciples played a role in this miracle too.

Lazarus was bound hand and foot with grave clothes, and his face had
been wrapped with a cloth during his time in the tomb. When he arose from
his death and came out of the tomb, Jesus called on the disciples to help in
the transformation process.
Jesus said to them, "Take off
the grave clothes and let him
go." The disciples needed to
help Lazarus. Likewise, we all
have a part to play in the lives
of those around us.

> When it comes to the
> transforming power of God
> working in someone's life, God
> often uses people to bring
> about divine life change.

God has done some in-
credible things around us during this fast. Could it be that someone around
you is still walking around in grave clothes? What do you need to help him
or her let go of?

Talking to men for God is a great thing, but talking to God for men is greater still. —E. M. BOUNDS

True prayer is measured by weight—not by length. A single groan before God may have more fullness of prayer in it than a fine oration of great length.
—CHARLES H. SPURGEON

Bible Reading Plan: Luke 12

Prayer Focus: Who in your world is still walking around in grave clothes? Think about friends and family or those you know who may not know God. What part has God called you to play in the life change He wants to bring them?

Optional Book Reading Plan: Chapter 8, beginning at page 75 ("Alignment") and stopping at page 81 ("Assignment")

The Awakening Journey

_____

_____

_____

_____

_____

_____

_____

_____

_____

Humility

> And when they had come to the multitude, a man came to
> Him, kneeling down to Him and saying, "Lord, have mercy
> on my son, for he is an epileptic and suffers severely; for he
> often falls into the fire and often into the water. So I brought
> him to Your disciples, but they could not cure him."
>
> —MATTHEW 17:14–16

W HAT A GREAT EXAMPLE OF HUMILITY: this man approached
Jesus and knelt before Him in the midst of a crowd. As the father
approached, he believed that Jesus would bring his son relief. But even in his
belief, his approach was humble and submitted to what Christ would choose
to do.

Looking further into the story, we
find the father was also persistent and
resisted taking offense. Though the disciples were not able to help him, he set
aside his temporary disappointment in
their failure and continued to seek after
Jesus—the solution to his circumstance, the source of relief through his trial.

> Approaching God with
> a heart of humility will
> always position you to
> find relief in Jesus.

Being humble before God is realizing our need of Him, submitting to
His will, pursuing Him, and being confident the outcome will occur in
God's perfect timing.

Be encouraged that approaching God with a heart of humility will always position you to find relief in Jesus. Don't be ashamed to humble yourself before God, even in the presence of others. Though offenses and disappointments may come, continue in your pursuit of Jesus. You may not get relief right away, but know this: *God is never late and His solution is always perfect!*

> *The higher a man is in grace, the lower he will be in his own esteem.* —CHARLES H. SPURGEON

Bible Reading Plan: Proverbs 2

Prayer Focus: Prayer is a posture of humility. Humble yourself before the Lord each day and bring your cares to Him. He wants to meet you where you are and answer your every need. Pray, too, that God will help you with the disappointment and discouragement that we all face along the way. Is there discouragement in your heart today? Write it down and release it to our perfect God.

Optional Book Reading Plan: Chapter 8, beginning at page 81 ("Assignment") through end of chapter

The Awakening Journey

_____

_____

_____

_____

_____

_____

_____

_____

Pray Instead

Don't fret or worry. Instead of worrying, pray. Let petitions
and praises shape your worries into prayers, letting God
know your concerns. Before you know it, a sense of God's
wholeness, everything coming together for good, will come
and settle you down. It's wonderful what happens when
Christ displaces worry at the center of your life.

—PHILIPPIANS 4:6–7, MSG

WORRY SEEMS INESCAPABLE IN MODERN LIFE. No doubt there
is plenty to worry about: our kids, the economy, global warming,
war, disease… Sometimes it might seem that worry has even replaced Jesus as
the focal point of our lives. Jesus Himself admonished us several times not to
worry. And the apostle Paul told us that there is an antidote to worry…prayer.

When we worry about something, we are spending energy on it, wonder-
ing what might happen, rehearsing the "if onlys" and "what ifs" in our mind.
Why not take that same energy
and refocus it on prayer instead? When we worry, we are
simply talking to ourselves
about our fears, but when we
pray, we are taking those fears
to God. We can't control the
future, but as Anne Graham

> Our timeless God owns the
> future. He knows exactly
> what is going to happen, and
> He promises to be with us
> every step of the journey.

Lotz said throughout her book *Fear Not Tomorrow, God Is Already There,* our timeless God owns the future. He knows exactly what is going to happen, and He promises to be with us every step of the journey.

As we are nearing a close to this season of prayer and fasting, let's heed Paul's words to "let petitions and praises shape your worries into prayers." Then the peace of God will guard your heart.

> *Growing an unshakable trust in God as you face your tomorrows is not about self-improvement or mastering your circumstances, but about God—who He is, what He does, and how we can trust Him.* —ANNE GRAHAM LOTZ

> *We have to pray with our eyes on God, not on the difficulties.* —OSWALD CHAMBERS

Bible Reading Plan: Luke 13

Prayer Focus: What consistently causes you to worry? Today, recapture each worried thought and send it to God as a prayer. See how dramatically your outlook improves when the peace of God is activated through prayer!

Optional Book Reading Plan: Chapter 9, pages 89–95 (stop at "The Sin Experience Versus the God Experience")

The Awakening Journey

_____

_____

_____

_____

_____

DAY 19 ☑

Walking in the Power of the Holy Spirit

Then Jesus returned in the power of the
Spirit to Galilee, and news of Him went
out through all the surrounding region.

—LUKE 4:14

AFTER PRAYING AND FASTING FOR FORTY DAYS, Jesus returned to Galilee empowered to do all the Father had called Him to do. Jesus was so powerful in public because He was so prayerful in private.

To accomplish the assignments God has for our lives, we also need the power of the Holy Spirit working in and through us. God does not expect us to go through the challenges of life without this power.

Prayer and fasting bring us to the place where we can power up. Walking in the power of the Holy Spirit is living with a comprehension of the God-given strength and authority in our lives to walk out His will.

> Jesus was so powerful in public because He was so prayerful in private.

Through prayer and fasting, God can prepare us for what lies ahead. We might not know what obstacles we're going to face, but we can know that God will be faithful to us. He will never leave us (Hebrews 13:5) and He will empower us to meet whatever challenges life may bring.

Every great movement of God can be traced to a kneeling figure. — D. L. MOODY

Bible Reading Plan: Luke 14

Prayer Focus: Today as you worship God in prayer, let Him know that you refuse to go into the future without His power and that you want all the spiritual resources He has for you.

Optional Book Reading Plan: Chapter 9, beginning at page 95 ("The Sin Experience Versus the God Experience") through end of chapter

The Awakening Journey

_____
_____
_____
_____
_____
_____
_____
_____
_____
_____
_____
_____
_____
_____
_____
_____
_____

A New Wineskin

And no one puts new wine into old wineskins. For
the new wine would burst the wineskins, spilling
the wine and ruining the skins. New wine must
be stored in new wineskins.

—LUKE 5:37–38, NLT

TWO THINGS THAT DO NOT MIX are *new wine* and *old wineskins.*
The reason is simple: old wineskins cannot grow and stretch to hold
the new wine.

The new wine God wants to fill you with is a picture of God's Spirit, and
this wine is expansive. A container that is dead, dry, stiff, and shrinking cannot be trusted as a storehouse for God's valued treasure. Our vessels must be
prepared for the fresh, dynamic, living presence of God, because everything
we do will flow from that.

This prepara-
tion comes through
prayer and fasting,
during which we
produce a container
that is ready for the

> God's new wine always changes us
> by expanding our faith, enlarging our
> purpose, and bringing renewed vision.

new thing God wants to do. God's new wine always changes us by expanding
our faith, enlarging our purpose, and bringing renewed vision.

God is not into old wineskins; it is up to us to shed them. As we seek Him in this season, let's shed the old wineskin and ask God to fully prepare our hearts for what's to come.

God became man to turn creatures into sons; not simply to produce better men of the old kind but to produce a new kind of man. — C. S. LEWIS

Bible Reading Plan: Psalms 8–9

Prayer Focus: What has caused you to shrink back in your expectation of what God wants to do in your life? Are you ready to be expanded beyond recognition? That's what God's new wine will do in and through you. Pray that the Lord will expand your life to glorify Him, giving you boldness to step out and be used by Him.

Optional Book Reading Plan: Chapter 10

The Awakening Journey

_____
_____
_____
_____
_____
_____
_____
_____
_____
_____
_____
_____

What's Your Assignment?

> Jesus, full of the Holy Spirit, returned from the Jordan
> and was led by the Spirit in the desert, where for forty
> days he was tempted by the devil. He ate nothing during
> those days, and at the end of them he was hungry.... Jesus
> returned to Galilee in the power of the Spirit, and news
> about him spread through the whole countryside. He
> taught in their synagogues, and everyone praised him.
>
> —LUKE 4:1–2, 14–15, NIV

FASTING AND PRAYER ARE ESSENTIAL to receiving a clear vision of God's specific path for our lives. Many times after a season of prayer and fasting we have a more defined understanding of the part we play in the body of Christ, as well as a greater sense of our particular spiritual giftings (1 Corinthians 12).

We learn a lot from observing the circumstances surrounding the beginning of Jesus' public ministry (Luke 4). Notice that He went into

> Fasting and prayer are essential to receiving a clear vision of God's specific path for our lives.

the desert "full of the Holy Spirit." However, He returned to Galilee "in the power of the Holy Spirit." Being full of the Spirit is to know God and His character; walking in the power of the Spirit is when we know that we have the God-given strength and authority in our lives to walk out His will.

The power of the Spirit is essential for us to accomplish the assignment God has for us. God could be leading you to fast so that you can receive His specific instructions for your life. He will equip you not just to know Him but to walk in His power to accomplish what He has called you to do.

That's exciting!

> *A man can no more take in a supply of grace for the future than he can eat enough today to last him for the next six months, or take sufficient air into his lungs at once to sustain life for a week to come. We must draw upon God's boundless stores of grace from day to day, as we need it.*
> —D. L. MOODY

Bible Reading Plan: Luke 15

Prayer Focus: Are there areas of your life that need more clarity? Are you walking in the power of the Spirit and living in God's purpose for your life? Write down those things God is speaking to you. As you conclude your fast, pray that God continually reveals His purpose and gives you ever-increasing clarity and strength to walk it out.

Optional Book Reading Plan: Chapter 12

The Awakening Journey

_____

_____

_____

_____

_____

_____

The Next Twenty-One Days

Never be lacking in zeal, but keep your spiritual
fervor, serving the Lord.
—ROMANS 12:11, NIV

I PRAY THAT THESE TWENTY-ONE DAYS have been an incredible experience for you. I also want to encourage you to be just as intentional about
the next twenty-one days…and the twenty-one days after that…and so on.
Keeping the fire and zeal for God burning in your heart is what will keep
your relationship with Him fresh and new. It will allow you to continue serving and obeying Him from a position of "want to," and you will experience
the joy of your salvation every day—regardless of what life brings your way.

The principles you have practiced in these twenty-one days are very easy
to sustain long term. Prayer, fasting, and personal devotion are all quite simple to incorporate into your everyday life. Over these last twenty-one days,
you've created space for God to fill. The best way to continue in these same
practices is to keep that space open indefinitely. Don't allow it to close up!
Protect that time and space with God and make it your priority each day.

Just like reading your Bible, praying, and attending church, fasting is also
a lifestyle. I encourage you to establish a frequency and consistency of fasting
in your life, as I have. Every January, I set aside twenty-one days to pray, fast,
and seek God. However, some years under the leading of the Holy Spirit, this
focused time could be thirty or forty days. After that I will fast one day a
week for the rest of the year. I fast an additional three consecutive days in the

spring, seven consecutive days in August—back-to-school time—and three consecutive days in November.

Remember, this is not a legalistic thing. This is an "I get to experience God" thing. It is like going into heaven for a tune-up, so I can keep my passion for God and enjoyment of Him at a high level. I encourage you to do the same. Figure out what works for you, commit to it, and make it a part of your life.

There is no doubt in my mind that as you followed the principles laid out in this book, you have experienced the presence of God in a powerful way.

> It is like going into heaven for a tune-up, so I can keep my passion for God and enjoyment of Him at a high level.

Every January at Celebration Church we receive hundreds of testimonies from people who have participated in Awakening: 21 Days of Prayer and Fasting. We hear about incredible moves of God, about people experiencing Him in a much more powerful way, and about all kinds of miracles and breakthroughs taking place as a by-product of people drawing closer to God. I shared a few of these with you in this book. They are an encouragement to me and to all who read them.

If you have a personal story you'd like to share, please e-mail or write me (see contact information at the end of the book). I'd love to hear about what God has done in your life through *Awakening*.

Remember, a lifestyle of passionate Christianity is supposed to be the norm, not the exception. Don't ever settle for less. Keep the fire for God burning in your heart and do what it takes to feed your spiritual hunger for God.

The tendency of fire is to go out; watch the fire on the altar of your heart. Anyone who has tended a fireplace fire knows that it needs to be stirred up occasionally.
—WILLIAM BOOTH

SMALL GROUP
STUDY GUIDE

WEEK ONE

Launch

In Matthew 9:15 Jesus said His disciples "will fast." Everything Jesus instructed us to do is purposeful, powerful, and effective. This being true...

1. In what ways do you think fasting could affect your relationship with God and His plans for your life?

Discussion

Fasting, when coupled with prayer, is one of the most powerful spiritual exercises we can engage in. Over time, the pressures of life, the weakness of our flesh, and just the day-to-day busyness of life itself can weigh us down, causing us to get out of sync with God and His plan for our lives. But fasting helps us hit the reset button, and draw closer to God (James 4:8).

2. What happens when we start to get out of line with God's will for our lives?
3. What are some of the warning signs you've experienced that indicate it's time to hit the reset button?

In Luke 4:1 when Jesus was led into the wilderness, the Bible said He was filled with the Holy Spirit. After forty days of fasting...

> Then Jesus returned in the power of the Spirit to Galilee, and news of Him went out through all the surrounding region. (Luke 4:14)

4. How would you describe what happened to Jesus as a result of His forty-day season of prayer and fasting?

Let's look at just one example of New Testament fasting:

> As they ministered to the Lord and fasted, the Holy Spirit said, "Now separate to Me Barnabas and Saul for the work to which I have called them." Then, having fasted and prayed, and laid hands on them, they sent them away. (Acts 13:2–3)

5. What were the results of this time of fasting and prayer?

It takes deliberate effort on our parts to remove any obstacles that come between us and God. Fasting cleanses our bodies and minds, making a way for God's supernatural, enabling power to flow freely into our lives again. It's like a spiritual overhaul.

Application

Jesus said "when you fast," not " if you fast." Fasting simplifies our lives, because as we draw closer to God, He brings our spiritual focus back in alignment with His will. It's like hitting the reset button both spiritually and physically. As we line up with the plans God has for us, He releases His enabling grace and power to carry them out.

Prayer

Share needs and requests and pray for one another.

WEEK TWO

Launch

How much does prayer really matter? How do I know God hears me when I pray? How can I know that God will say yes to my prayers? These are questions most of us ask at some point in life.

1. What question about prayer would you most like to have answered?

Discussion

James 5:16 says, "The effective, fervent prayer of a righteous man avails much."

2. What do the words *effective* and *fervent* mean to you?

When we accept Jesus as our Savior, we are made righteous in the eyes of God. When we pray, God wants us to approach Him with the confidence of knowing He loves and accepts us.

3. Do you believe some of your own issues or the way you behave keeps God from answering your prayers?

Jesus said, "If you abide in Me, and My words abide in you, you will ask what you desire, and it shall be done for you" (John 15:7). Based on this verse...

4. Can we pray whatever we want and know that God will do it? What is our role in prayer?
5. Generally speaking, when you pray, do you find you are praying for relief from some issue, or are you praying that God will be glorified?

6. Do you have the confidence that God hears your prayers? Why
    or why not?

Application

Take an inventory of your prayer life. It will be the most effective when it is
Bible based and grounded in a heart to glorify God. What adjustments can
you make in your life to spend more time seeking God?

Prayer

Close your time together by both bringing requests to God as well as seeking
to glorify Him with your prayers.

WEEK THREE

Launch

New Testament fasting is about drawing closer to God and coming into
alignment with Him. We do not fast to try and change God's mind; instead,
we are the ones changed.

1. How does New Testament fasting bring about a different kind
    of experience for us as we fast?

Discussion

Fasting brings us into full agreement with the will of God. As Jesus said while
teaching His disciples how to pray:

> In this manner, therefore, pray:
>   Our Father in heaven,
>   Hallowed be Your name.
>   Your kingdom come.
>   Your will be done
>   On earth as it is in heaven. (Matthew 6:9–10)

2. What is the meaning of the word *kingdom* in the Lord's Prayer?
3. When we fast, how will His kingdom come and His will be done in our lives?

Fasting creates a new wineskin. Matthew 9:14–17 reads:

Then the disciples of John came to Him, saying, "Why do we and the Pharisees fast often, but Your disciples do not fast?"

And Jesus said to them, "Can the friends of the bridegroom mourn as long as the bridegroom is with them? But the days will come when the bridegroom will be taken away from them, and then they will fast. No one puts a piece of unshrunk cloth on an old garment; for the patch pulls away from the garment, and the tear is made worse. Nor do they put new wine into old wineskins, or else the wineskins break, the wine is spilled, and the wineskins are ruined. But they put new wine into new wineskins, and both are preserved."

4. What might a new wineskin represent in our personal lives?
5. How can aligning ourselves with God through fasting bring about a change in our lives and leave us transformed by the Holy Spirit?

Fasting and praying brings us into a place of assignment.

6. Jesus fasted and prayed for forty days (Luke 4:1–13). What did this experience prepare Him for when He walked out of the wilderness?
7. If we follow the example of Jesus, what do you think God is calling us to do in preparation for His assignment to be carried out in our lives?

Application

Prayer and fasting recommit us to the lordship of Christ where we can walk in agreement with His will, in alignment with an open heaven, and confident that He will give us the grace, strength, and wisdom to carry out our divine assignment.

Prayer

Together offer prayers of thanksgiving for what God has done—and will do—because of this twenty-one-day fast.

ACKNOWLEDGMENTS

To my lovely wife, Kerri, for everything you add to my life. Thank you for your constant support and encouragement. I am so grateful for you.

To my wonderful children, Kaylan, Stovie, and Annabelle. You bring me so much joy. I love being your dad.

To Linda Riddle, for your contribution to *Awakening* and for your commitment and enthusiasm to see it through every step of the way.

To Jeff Dunn, for your research and helpful insight during those formative days. I appreciate you and am thankful for your help.

ABOUT THE AUTHOR

STOVALL WEEMS is the founder and lead pastor of Celebration Church in Jacksonville, Florida, one of the fastest growing and largest churches in America. Celebration Church is a global, diverse, multisite church that reaches people from all walks of life. Since it began with just seven people in 1998, the church has grown both regionally and internationally to twelve locations with over ten thousand people in weekend attendance.

Stovall is noted for his energetic, engaging, and practical communication style. As pastor, teacher, and conference speaker, his ministry focuses on building the local church, reaching people with the gospel, and developing passionate followers of Christ.

Stovall is also the leader of Awakening, a twenty-one-day spiritual campaign of prayer and fasting that takes place each January. Awakening serves to equip thousands of pastors, churches, and ministry leaders around the world, inspiring a culture of prayer and fasting in their churches and ministries.

Stovall and his wife, Kerri, have three children, Kaylan, Stovie, and Annabelle.

JOIN WITH OVER 1 MILLION OTHER PARTICIPANTS!

Awakening:
21 Days of Prayer, Fasting & Personal Devotion
January

Led by Pastor Stovall Weems, the goal of Awakening is three-fold:

Inspire

pastors, churches, and ministry leaders to establish or strengthen a
culture of prayer and fasting in their local church or ministry.

Equip

pastors, churches, and ministry leaders with resources and tools that can
help facilitate a successful season of prayer and fasting in their community.

Pray

and fast together at the onset of the year to position our churches and
leadership for maximum effectiveness in the coming year.

To find out more and register for resources,
visit **Awake21.org.**